# WOMEN'S REALITY
## An Emerging Female System
## in the White Male Society
### Anne Wilson Schaef

WINSTON PRESS

D0167833

*Connolly*

Cover Design: Kathe Wilcoxon

Library of Congress Catalog Card Number: 80-53560

Printed in the United States of America.

5 4 3 2

Winston Press, Inc.
430 Oak Grove
Minneapolis, Minnesota 55403

# ACKNOWLEDGMENTS

I want to thank all of the women and men who have supported my work, and with their lives and struggles have lived the material presented here.

Ann Sprague, Vonna Moody and Jill Schumacher spent hours typing and retyping the manuscript with no pay but their eagerness for this book to come into being. Carol Pearson constantly reminded me that I could be a writer and added her many writing and editing skills to the process. Without her help, I never could have "done a book."

Lastly, the greatest surprise in the process was my editor, Pamela Espeland, who is a strong woman skilled at her craft.

*It is not necessary*
*to deny another's reality*
*in order to affirm my own.*

To women—all who have helped me learn; to femaleness, which I have come to love by seeking to understand it; to my clients and my friends, who are frequently one and the same.

To Male Chauvinist Pigs—with whom I have been intimately related; to other men who fill in the gaps left by those in the White Male System.

And most of all to my family, which continues to bring me into being.

# Contents

# PREFACE

This book is about a reality—a reality perceived, explored, and expressed by women whenever they are free to do so without fear. It is about who we are as women. When we understand and accept who we are, we become in turn more understandable and accepted.

This book has three purposes: liberation, sharing, and communication. It is intended to liberate women from an unnecessary oppression based on myths. It is intended to share and legitimate what all women know—some of which they are willing to admit to themselves, and some of which they are willing to admit to others. It is intended to communicate in the "female idiom." Women rarely have an opportunity to read a book written in their idiom. This experience is important for self-validation and growth. It is important to the development of self-esteem and self-worth. Since women live in a foreign culture, they seldom have the experience of receiving approval and validation by the "authorities"—people whose ideas and opinions appear in print. That is the gift of this book. Simply because it exists, it validates and confirms femaleness in this culture. It expresses a reality of which many women know but are not always aware—that of being *in* a culture but not *of* it.

I wrote this book because I had to. Much of it is not new or even original; rather, it is the result of other voices speaking through me. I have spent over a decade listening to women—and men—in intense situations, including individual therapy sessions, groups, and workshops, and this book embodies many of the things they have thought and said. The material in it has come together slowly over a period of years. I have presented parts of it in various forms around the United States and Canada, and it has become an affirmation to women—and men—of their experience in this culture and what it means.

I think it is important to note that during the time I was gathering the information for this book, I did not read any of the literature of the psychology of women or books of the women's movement because I did not want to be influenced by the ideas of others. After I put the concepts together, I read widely in women's literature and discovered an impressive convergence of ideas.

We are all engaged in a long and difficult process of *growth* and evolution. It is time to describe, affirm, and *grow*. This book is a stepping-stone in that process. In it, I have attempted to appreciate and affirm the intellect while also valuing and enhancing those other parts of being which nonfiction traditionally ignores—concepts, feelings, experiences, intuition, and awareness.

This book attempts to speak to the soul as well as the mind. It takes the responsibility of expressing that which demands expression.

Anne Wilson Schaef   1981

# FOREWORD

About twelve years ago, I went into private practice as a psychotherapist. As more and more women came to see me, it became clear to me that I did not know what to do with them. (This phenomenon is not unusual for persons in private practice, but admitting it is!) As I reviewed my training, I began to realize that what I had been taught was useful in working with *men* but at best useless and at worst harmful in working with *women*.

I decided to set aside a period of my life to learn about women. (Since I am one myself, this commitment had decided personal advantages!) I determined to clear my mind of past attitudes and assumptions as much as possible and take time to watch and listen. Fortunately, I was in a position to gather a great deal of relevant information. I was seeing several individual clients. I was conducting a number of groups, and I was consulting with many organizations in a variety of ways— facilitating encounter groups; doing organizational consulting, group process training, and educational consulting; and acting as a management and program consultant.

I had countless opportunities to enter a group situation and set the tone. As often as I was able, I met with groups composed exclusively of women. These included encounter workshops, group process workshops, church groups, PTA's, professional women's groups, and women's workshops. I spoke with adolescents, senior citizens, and women of all ages in between. Although the majority belonged to the white middle class, others were Black, Chicana, or Native American. Almost all of the women I saw were working women both in and outside the home.

I focused on making each encounter safe, nonjudgmental, and candid so that the women could express their own perceptions and reveal themselves without fear of reprisal. Along the way, I collected, revised, and expanded the material contained in this book.

The research I did is generally classified under the heading, "soft research." Margaret Mead and Sigmund Freud were both good examples of "soft researchers"—data-gatherers who watch and listen. When engaged in this type of study, one begins to see and hear the same information from many different people in many different situations. One begins to draw generalizations. The generalizations start coming together to give birth to concepts. The concepts cluster and evolve into theories.

In other words, the theory explored here resulted from *synthesis*, not *analysis*. I emphasize this point because it is essential to an understanding of this book. The generalizations and concepts which contributed to the formation of this theory came from women with whom I met both individually and collectively. They came up against, melted into, and joined with generalizations and concepts of my own. I hope that this theory helps us to conceptualize and understand what it means to be female in our culture; I hope it helps us to develop a language that will enable us to communicate our experience. In this way, we will open an avenue for mutual understanding and empathy.

Understanding is my goal. It offers the opportunity for further growth and change. Growth and change are normal to the human condition. When we define their courses and objectives, however, we limit them and ourselves. All I do here is to describe. As I describe, you will understand; as you understand, growth and change will occur. I do not want to control the course or objectives of your personal change.

Far too frequently, I have seen psychotherapists and social scientists use theory as a weapon. They have been trained in certain theories, and they have come to accept and believe in them. Because of this, they try to make their clients conform to their theories, regardless of what their clients really need.

I feel that this practice, while admittedly an occupational hazard among therapists and social scientists, is grossly unfair to clients. I see theory as a *tool* we can use to help us explain and conceptualize. When a particular theory fits a particular observation, we should go ahead and use it. When it does not, we should throw the theory out! Theory is only useful within its limitations; no one theory explains everything. Our most productive opportunities for new growth and understanding may come during times when our theory just does not work. Only when we can relieve ourselves of the responsibility of knowing and understanding everything, can we be open to true expansion of knowledge. Theory can either add to our knowledge or limit it by causing us to overlook important information. It all depends on how we use it.

I am concerned that the theory presented here not be used as a weapon against women. I have already seen that happening. While retraining therapists to work with women, I have met several who are genuinely eager to understand and be helpful. They have listened with great interest and taken voluminous notes at my workshops. Then they have gone off and told their women clients in subtle yet direct ways what they should be feeling, thinking, and working on. This misuse of theory frightens and angers me. I implore anyone who reads this book not to use its contents to demonstrate superiority or be "one up." Nor should anyone use it in an attempt to "raise the consciousness" of his or her spouse. Leave this process to a friend or outside source. Relationships are difficult enough to maintain as is!

This is *not* a "how-to" book. Its purpose is not to tell women how to behave, nor is it to tell private practitioners how to treat their clients. Instead, the observations and concepts presented here can best be used to help us all be less ignorant. Theory is most useful when it affords us the opportunity to see what we otherwise might miss and follow that up in our work and personal lives. Ideally, theory remains in the unconscious or preconscious until triggered by a real event. It emerges to serve its function—that of helping one to explain and understand.

By no means does this book present the complete picture. At times, I have found this personally frustrating. I have felt as if I should wait to begin writing, or wait to add more to this book, until I understood it all. That, of course, is not possible, so I decided to stop waiting for that day to come. If I succeed in clarifying even the smallest part of who women are and what it means to be female in our culture, I will ask nothing more.

Some women will not agree with, or will not have experienced, everything described here. I do not expect everyone to agree with this book. It is intended to facilitate growth, and it very well may end up generating some conflict along the way. That will be just fine with me.

If there is something you simply cannot accept or live with, ignore it. Do not judge yourself in terms of others' experiences or opinions. I have found that there is almost always *something* in this material that strikes a resonant chord in every woman. Take from this book only that which seems useful to you. Do not feel the need to reject yourself or this material if everything does not "fit." Take what is yours, and leave the rest!

Women often feel threatened if they are labeled "different." We frequently find ourselves behaving or believing differently from what an "authority" tells us is the "right" way. In the Female System, there is not right or wrong. It is possible to be different and still be all right. There can be two—or more—answers to the same question, and all can be right. None has to be wrong. Check out for yourself which of these ideas and concepts fits for you. If you come across something that does not seem useful or relevant to you, put it on a back burner and go on to something else.

Men may have some difficulty understanding this material. I have found that Black, Chicano, Native American, and Asian-American men generally have an easier time of it than white men, however. If you are male and cannot understand certain parts of this book, discuss them with five women, three of whom are feminists. If after that you still cannot understand or accept these ideas, then you may have a great deal of work left to do. Please remember that when one person tries to explain her or his system to another, it usually takes twice as much energy for her or him to develop and present an explanation as it does for the listener to understand it.

Two Female Systems are presented in this book. The first is a reactive system. It is not a system that women would choose but is a way of coping with the roles and places assigned to women by the White Male System. As a reactive system, it is neither tight nor cohesive; rather, it reflects a series of dilemmas and strategies for living within the structures of the White Male System.

The other Female System is discussed in relation to similar elements in the White Male System. This Female System is one that emerges when women "get clear" and feel free to express their values and perceptions. This Female System is much more coherent and cohesive than the elements of the reactive female system discussed earlier in the book. This emerging system is what can more truly be described as *The* Female System.

While reading this book, it is important to remember that the Female System is variable and changing. It is a system in process and is in itself a process. It is an open-ended system. The White Male System, on the other hand, is a closed system. It is logical to expect that as sex roles change and become clearer, persons of both sexes will get better at understanding and respecting both systems, the systems will change, and dichotomies between them may even be eliminated.

The concepts and theories presented here are philosophical, psychological, sociological, political, and theological. My purpose in writing this book was to present them in such a way that all of us may begin to develop a deeper understanding and awareness of our culture and perhaps even act on that understanding and awareness. I believe that as we begin to notice, label, and conceptualize, we can also begin to learn and to grow.

I have found that the concepts of the Female System and the White Male System have helped men as well as women. Many men I know have responded to these theories with support and relief at finally hearing them verbalized.

It is important to say that there is a Female System. It is not bad or good; it just is. It is important to acknowledge its existence.

CHAPTER ONE

# FITTING IN: THE WHITE MALE SYSTEM AND OTHER SYSTEMS IN OUR CULTURE

## THE WHITE MALE SYSTEM AND THE WAY THE WORLD ISN'T

When working with clients, therapists have traditionally taken one of two approaches: the *intrapsychic* or the *interpersonal.* In the former, the therapist focuses on what goes on *inside* the person, emphasizing the importance of dreams, fantasies, defense mechanisms, fixations, and the like. Of special significance are the first five years of a client's life; these are seen as having shaped the person and determined what she or he would be and become in the future.

Many practitioners now feel that the intrapsychic approach is sorely lacking. The information gained by that methodology may be useful, but it is just not enough. True, a therapist can work with an individual's insides and make great strides, but it is also necessary to work with her or his *outsides*—specifically, to become aware of and/or involved with the significant others in the client's life. After all, no one lives in a vacuum! The interpersonal approach, then, focuses on the system in which the client lives *and* on the system which is the client herself or himself.

As a practicing psychotherapist, I myself have used both approaches—the intrapsychic and the interpersonal—with my clients, depending on their needs and my perceptions. Both have worked at different times; both have helped people to become living, loving, capable individuals. Still, I have never been entirely satisfied with either approach or the combination of the two. Something is missing from each one—something which I have grown to feel is essential not only to the therapeutic process but also to getting along in the world on a day-to-day basis.

What is missing is an understanding and awareness of what I have chosen to call the White Male System. It is crucial to be able to define this system and deal with it simply because it surrounds us and permeates our lives. Its myths, beliefs, rituals, procedures, and outcomes affect everything we think, feel, and do.

Let me explain what I mean by the White Male System. It is the system in which we live, and in it, the power and influence are held by white males. This system did not happen overnight, nor was it the result of the machinations of only a few individuals; we all not only let it occur but participated in its development. Nevertheless, the White Male System is just that: a system. We all live in it, but it is not reality. It is not the way the world is. Unfortunately, some of us do not recognize that it is a system and think it *is* reality or the way the world is.

The White Male System—and it is important to keep in mind that I am referring to a *system* here and not pointing a finger at specific individuals within it—controls almost every aspect of our culture. It makes our laws, runs our economy, sets our salaries, and decides when and if we will go to war or remain at home. It decides what *is* knowledge and how it is to be taught. Like any other system, it has both positive and negative qualities. But because it is only a system, it can be clarified, examined, and changed, both from within and without.

There are other systems within our culture. The

Black System, the Chicano System, the Asian-American System, and the Native American System are completely enveloped in and frequently overshadowed by the White Male System. As, of course, is the Female System, which includes women from the other ethnic systems as well as white women.

There are a few white men who do not fit into the White Male System. They form a small but growing group which is frequently perceived as a sanctuary by white men who do not want to acknowledge their sexism. Whenever I mention the existence of this group during a lecture, I can almost see the men in the room rushing to crowd into it. If they can just get into that circle, they can be "different" and not have to face themselves. I wait until they are comfortably crowded in before saying, "Of course, at this point in history that group is largely homosexual." They then quickly rush right out again! I use this statement for effect, and while it is not necessarily accurate, it *does* encourage men to realize that there is more to sexism than meets the eye. This keeps the focus where it should be and is also an amusing process to observe.

Saying that you are not sexist—or that you do not want to be, or would rather not admit that you are—is not the same as doing something about your sexism. To give a parallel example, this is much like what many of us white liberals did during the civil rights movement. We needed our Black friends to tell us that we were different. We needed to hear that we were not like everyone else, that we were not discriminatory and racist. Once we heard that, we could avoid having to deal with our racism, which was real no matter how hard we tried to ignore it or cover it up.

I had two Black colleagues who simply refused to tell me what I wanted to hear. I finally learned that the issue was not one of *whether* I was racist, but of *how* I was racist. As soon as I was able to acknowledge this—with my friends' help—then and only then could I begin to work on my own racist attitudes and behaviors. Similarly, because we all live in a white male culture, the question is not one of *whether* we are sexist, but of *how* we are sexist. (This is true for women as well as men, by the way.)

Before we can deal with our sexism, we must learn to distance ourselves from the White Male System. We must learn to step back, take a long look at it, and see it for what it really is.

## CLEARING THE AIR: POLLUTION VS. NON-POLLUTION

I like to think of the White Male System as analogous to pollution. When you are in the middle of pollution, you are usually unaware of it (unless it is especially bad.) You eat in it, sleep in it, work in it, and sooner or later start believing that that is just the way the air is. You are unaware of the fact that pollution is *not* natural until you remove yourself from it and experience non-pollution.

I live in the Colorado mountains where the air is very clear. Whenever I go to the East Coast, I almost immediately start coughing and fighting a post-nasal drip. As I choke and sputter, I comment to local residents, "My, the pollution is bad today!" They in turn look startled and ask, "What pollution?" What they are really saying, of course, is this: "Isn't the air always a little thick and yellowish-gray?"

When flying into New York—or Los Angeles, for that matter—it is easy enough to look down and say, "Now, that's pollution!" Once you are in it for a while, though, you simply forget all about it and accept polluted air as a given.

Native Americans have always recognized the White Male System as pollution. The Blacks were the next group to challenge the system. The Blacks went off by themselves and said, "We have a system of our own—the Black system. It isn't always right, but it isn't always wrong. Black is beautiful and our system is just fine." Until then, very few groups had stepped away from the White Male System, reflected on it, and declared their own alternatives.

It is very difficult to stand back from the White Male System because it is everywhere in our culture. You can get away from pollution by leaving New York City and going to the mountains, but you can not get away from the White Male System as easily as that. It *is* our culture. We all live in it. We have been educationally, politically, economically, philosophically, and theologically trained in it, and our emotional, psychological, physical, and spiritual survival have depended on our knowing and supporting the system. White women believe that they get their identity externally from the White Male System and that the White Male System is necessary to validate that identity. Therefore, challenging the system becomes almost impossible.

There is a direct correlation between buying into the White Male System and surviving in our culture. Since white women have bought into the system the most, they have survived better than other groups both economically and physically although they do get battered and raped and mutilated (for example, through unnecessary surgery). They have had to hide and/or unlearn their own system and accept the stereotypes that the White Male System has set up for them.

Blacks have accepted the White Male System less wholeheartedly than white women and have not done as well within it. (Of course, white men have not exactly been enthusiastic about welcoming Blacks into their system.) Chicanos and Asian Americans are even further removed. Finally, most Native Americans have generally refused to have anything at all to do with it. When one looks at how Native Americans have fared within this culture, one sees graphic evidence of what happens to those who try to escape or ignore the White Male System. They are either exterminated outright or have to fight every step of the way. Economic and physical survival have been directly related to accepting and incorporating the White Male System.

There is also an *inverse* relationship between accepting and incorporating the White Male System and personal survival. The stress of having to be innately superior at all times is more than the human organism can tolerate. Those persons who buy into the system the most and work the hardest to become shining examples of what it means tend to drop dead ahead of their time from heart attacks, strokes, high blood pressure, ulcers, and other physical after effects of unrelenting tension and stress.

One unforeseen consequence of the civil rights movement is that more Black males are dying of heart attacks these days. As they move into the White Male System and become part of it, they inherit the unfortunate legacy of stress and early death. The same appears to be true for women who are "making it" in the White Male System. It seems as if high blood pressure goes hand in hand with three-piece suits and attaché cases.

This does not have to be so, however. One big problem with the White Male System is that stress is assumed to be an integral part of the system. If one tries to live up to the myths of the system, then one naturally undergoes a great deal of strain. One can choose *not* to live up to these myths. One can choose to remove the causes of stress rather than merely learning how to cope with them. The only really effective way to go about doing this is to challenge the myths of the White Male System and eventually to change the system itself. It can be done; in some cases, it *is* already being done.

I am not talking here about women's liberation, or Black liberation, or the liberation of any other single group within our culture. Instead, I am looking forward to a time when we can all become the persons we really are. Blacks and women are learning to tell the difference between pollution and non-pollution. They are showing us that it is possible to stand back and say, "The White Male System is only a system. It is not reality. It is not the way the world is." Blacks have defined their own system, and some of them have tried to communicate this to the rest of us. Unfortunately, many of us have been very slow learners. It is difficult to teach a new concept to someone who already "knows it all" (one of the myths of the White Male System). Some Blacks have not bothered trying to tell others about their system. They have just focused on getting into the White Male System because they know they must in order to survive.

I have described the White Male System as it is perceived by Female System women. Similarly, there is a Female System. It is not good or bad. It just is. It is not necessary to choose one system over the other. As the Female System is described, we will see and understand another system. The more systems we know about, the more choices we have. Over time, perhaps, more new—and better—systems, models, and alternatives will emerge.

## THE FOUR GREAT MYTHS OF THE WHITE MALE SYSTEM

The White Male System has four myths that feed it, sustain it, and (theoretically at least) justify it. These myths have been around for so long that most men are not even conscious of them. Many would deny their existence. Yet to challenge or doubt them is akin to heresy: they are sacred givens.

The first myth is that *the White Male System is the only thing that exists.* Because of this, the beliefs and perceptions of other systems—especially the Female System—are seen as sick, bad, crazy, stupid, ugly, and incompetent.

This myth is damaging in two ways. It limits women who want to explore their own perceptions and abilities, and it limits men who want to experience and learn from them.

Almost every woman has heard these words more than once: "You just don't know how the world is!" implying that the White Male System's view of the world is somehow "right." Women are also told time and again that they do not understand "reality." The White Male System is not reality. It is *a* reality, but it is not *the* reality, and women may very well have a reality all their own. Neither reality is right. Neither is the way the world is. Each simply *is.* When one is set up as being the only true reality, however, and the other is dismissed as sick, bad, crazy, stupid, etc., then no one is free to explore the possibilities inherent in other realities.

There may be one true reality somewhere, but it has not yet been demonstrated that the White Male System can claim it. If we were all given the opportunity to seek out and study other realities, we might come closer to understanding one another. The myth which states that there is one and only one reality limits our search for others.

Since the White Male System is so thoroughly convinced that it is the only thing that exists in the world, it lacks what I like to call a "theology of differences." Once someone is sure that the way in which he (or she) sees the world is the way things *are,* then he (or she) perceives any differences of opinion as threatening. This results in a closed system and a rigid approach to life in which all differences must be discounted, disparaged, or destroyed. No one is allowed to explore them or use them as opportunities for new growth because their very existence jeopardizes the most basic myth of the White Male System—that it is the right and only way of life without which there would be nothing.

The second myth is that *the White Male System is innately superior.* Note that the first and second myths do not follow logically. If the White Male System is the only thing that exists, then how can it be superior and to what? Unfortunately, this inconsistency is of no concern to the White Male System.

At some level, the White Male System has recognized in spite of itself that other realities exist. It has gone on to define itself as superior to them while simultaneously believing that it is the only reality. Anyone who does not belong to this system is by definition innately inferior—and this includes members of all other racial groups, women, and the few white men who do not fit into the White Male System.

According to the White Male System, innate superiority and innate inferiority are birthrights which cannot be earned or traded away. Some men would like to give their innate superiority away—it is often too large a burden to bear. It is just plain difficult to be "the best" all of the time. Nor is it good for one's health. Superiority can be a killing gift.

The third myth is that *the White Male System knows and understands everything.* This is one reason why women so frequently look to men for advice and direction. Both sexes genuinely believe that men should and do know it all. In contrast to the first two myths, which are diametrically opposed, this myth follows the second one very nicely. If one is innately superior, then by rights one should be omniscient as well.

This myth is directly related to racial and sex-role stereotyping. A stereotype is no more than a definition of one group of persons by another who wishes to control it. Taken together, stereotypes support the myths of the White Male System.

No one would deny the fact that there are other people in our culture besides white men. Blacks, Chicanos, Native Americans, Asian Americans, and women are not exactly invisible. Precisely because they are different from white men, the White Male System must come to terms with them in some way. So it develops stereotypes that neatly describe and categorize these other groups. As long as the members of these groups go along with the stereotypes, they support the illusion that the White Male System knows and understands everything. If white men say that women are weak, and women behave as if they are weak, then who can argue with the myth?

Blacks were the first to defy the stereotypes given them by the White Male System. They started living within their own system. The other racial groups, and women, have done this also to some extent, but at considerable personal expense and threat to their existence.

The fourth and final myth of the White Male System is that *it is possible to be totally logical, rational, and objective.* The problem with this myth is that one must constantly do battle with the ways in which one is not all of these things. One must continually overcome and deny any tendencies toward illogical, irrational, subjective, or intuitive thoughts or behaviors.

Members of the White Male System spend a lot of time and energy telling women that females are by nature not logical, rational, or objective. Often they do so in highly emotional ways!

I once counseled with a couple who had marital problems. Both the man and the woman had thriving businesses of their own. The man was constantly complaining that while he was always logical and rational about their differences of opinion, his wife was always emotional. To support his position, he drafted a twenty-four-page document—on legal-sized paper—explaining the situation as he perceived it. He then presented it to me at the beginning of one session and told me to read it. During his next visit, he asked if I had understood his thesis. I told him that I had read the whole thing, carefully weighed it (literally!), and had come to the conclusion that any outpouring of that size and intensity had to be an emotional statement!

One part of psychology is the science of individual differences. Whole fields of study have developed out of the awareness that when two or more persons observe the same event, they are apt to come up with two or more different reports of it. People are simply not capable of being totally logical, rational, and objective.

The fourth myth—that this sort of behavior *is* possible—poses an occupational hazard for therapists (and their clients). If one accepts it, then one must neglect the subjective, intuitive resources within oneself. The therapeutic process becomes a problem to be solved in a series of logical, orderly steps rather than a healing experience. And a great deal of valuable data and information are lost along the way.

Living according to these myths can mean living in ignorance. For example, the only way to maintain the myth of knowing and understanding everything is to *ignore* a whole universe of other information. When one clings to the myth of innate superiority, one must constantly overlook the virtues and abilities of others.

Nevertheless, the mere thought that these myths might not be truisms terrifies White Male System persons. I have seen proof of this over and over again. Once, when I was lecturing on this subject to a group of professional men and women, I noticed one of the men

becoming increasingly agitated. When he could sit
still no longer (he started pacing back and forth at the
far end of the room), I finally stopped and asked him to
tell us what he was experiencing.

"If what you are saying is true," he said, "then I am
nothing but a piece of shit."

"I don't think I was implying that," I answered.
"Can you tell us more?"

"Well," he went on—and these were his exact
words—"if I'm not innately superior and I don't know
and understand everything, then I'm nothing but a
piece of shit, *just like the rest of you!*"

His statement suggests a number of important
issues. First, was his overwhelming need to hold on to
his sense of superiority and his conviction that he knew
and understood everything. Second, was his very real
fear that if this turned out not to be true, the only
alternative was to be worthless (like the rest of us)! This
reveals the dualistic thinking inherent in the White
Male System. Things have to be either this way or that.
One must be either superior or inferior. One must be
either one-up or one-down. What horrible and
debilitating options! How limiting and exhausting always
to have to be one-up so as not to be one-down.
Another assumption that his statement reveals is that
the only way the world can be is the way he sees it. If it
suddenly became different, then chaos would reign. It is
easy to see why men would be frightened by this. To
avoid this dreadful possibility, the White Male System
must defend itself at all costs and can not risk exploring
other alternatives.

A professional man became very upset during
another group I was leading. He stood up, waved his
arms, and said, "Anne, if you ever do get the power,
you'll do the same thing to us that we've done to you!"
What he was really saying, of course, was that power
could only be used as his system has used it—to control,

condemn, and stereotype. He was locked into his mythology. It is difficult for others of us to recognize how deeply this belief system penetrates the souls of white males and how frightening it is to have it challenged.

The White Male System sees its mythology as all-knowing and all-revealing. In truth, however, it is just the opposite. I realized this most clearly many years ago when I was doing a workshop on racial issues in a Southern state. (This was during the heyday of the civil rights movement, when school districts were required to sponsor workshops on this topic in order to keep their public funding.) The group I was working with was about half Blacks and half whites. Neither side wanted to disturb the tenuous equilibrium they had established thus far, and they invited me in because I was perceived as essentially harmless.

I had designed a relatively simple exercise I wanted to try out on the group in order to generate some data. I asked the participants to draw three columns on a sheet of paper. In the first, they were to list those characteristics which they perceived as uniquely Black. In the second, they were to list those they perceived as uniquely white. In the third, they were to list characteristics they saw as common to both groups.

After explaining what I wanted the group to do, I sat down to wait. After a while, the anxiety in the room became almost palpable. I decided to find out what was happening.

I found that the Blacks had done precisely what I had asked them to do. Because they knew the Black system, they had been able to list characteristics they perceived as uniquely Black. Because they also knew the White Male System—they had to in order to survive—they had been able to list characteristics they saw as uniquely white. They were ready to move on to the third column.

The whites were having great difficulty completing the exercise, however. Because they knew nothing about the Black system, they could not do column one. Because they could not see the White Male System for what it is (one has to experience non-pollution before being able to recognize pollution), they could not do column two either. Increasingly frustrated, most of them had gone directly to column three. They had decided to ignore the differences between the two systems ("Let's not look at differences. Differences separate us!") and focus instead on common characteristics ("Let's look at ways in which we're alike and ignore the experience of being Black in the White Male System!").

In addition, as often happens in educational groups, the whole group had started cheating. People were looking at one another's papers. When the whites saw that the Blacks had been able to come up with answers for the first two columns, they became agitated ("What do they know that we don't know—and how can this be?"). When the Blacks saw that the whites had not been able to come up with answers for those two columns, they felt exposed. ("We cannot let them know that *we* know that *they* don't know *more*. We'll lose our jobs if they find that we know they aren't superior.")

What the group had just experienced was a full-fledged myth-breaker. The whites were not superior and did not know more than the Blacks. In fact, the Blacks knew more. They had to. They had learned all about the White Male System because they needed to in order to survive in it. Because the whites did not have to know the Black system to survive, the whites had learned little or nothing about the Black system. The only way for them to find out about it would have been for Blacks to teach it to them, and that had not happened. Nor was it likely to happen.

Both sides were exhausted by this exercise. The whites were supposed to be innately superior and all-knowing—but they could not come up with answers! The Blacks were trying to support the myth that whites were innately superior and all-knowing—in order to keep· their jobs—but they had completed the exercise. Sometimes it is difficult to remember what one is not supposed to know! The myth was that the whites knew more. The reality was that the Blacks did.

Teaching a white man about a system other than his own can be extraordinarily difficult. Even if he is open to learning about other realities, he must constantly do battle with his own feeling of innate superiority and the confidence that he already knows and understands everything. These myths go deep into the core of most white males and are not easily overcome. It requires almost superhuman effort and enormous commitment on both sides. Now that I have been trying to teach the Female System to white men, I find myself appreciating the time, energy, and love my Black friends have put forth in teaching me about their system.

All four myths of the White Male System can be summarized by another that is almost always unspoken but nevertheless present and real. This final myth is that *it is possible for one to be God.* If the White Male System is the only system that exists, if white males are innately superior, if they know and understand everything, and if they can be totally logical, rational and objective, then they can be God—at least, the way the White Male System defines God.

Being a deity is not easy though. In fact, it can be lethal for White Male System persons to deny their own humanity and fallibility. The human mind and body are not designed to stand up under such stress and strain. White men who finally achieve such high stature in their own minds suffer from heart attacks, strokes, ulcers, and high blood pressure. In the end, godhood can kill.

# RELIGION, MATHEMATICS, AND THE WHITE MALE SYSTEM

The White Male System has its own religious belief system. While the four great myths and the belief that men can be God are at its core, there is far more to it than that. Its priests carry out the rituals, and its laymen are assigned to see that the system keeps running smoothly. This religion is the Scientific Method. If one adheres to its beliefs and follows its rituals and procedures, one can "prove" or "disprove" anything *within the system.*

Like most religions, the scientific method attempts to describe our universe and our lives in a way that "makes sense." It aims at understanding and explaining the worlds within and around us. It has gone beyond these goals, however, to reach a rather astonishing conclusion: *that it is possible to control the universe.* Most other religions attempt to comprehend the universe so that people can learn to live within it; the Native American belief systems are good examples of this. The White Male System does not want to live within the universe, though, but to run it!

We are all told at some point during our education that anything can be measured. All that is necessary is an awareness of which measurement or tool to use at a particular time. Measurement is seen as the key to success. If we can measure, we can predict. If we can predict, we can control. If we can control, we can be God. The White Male System believes that total mastery over the universe will come through better technology and better measurement techniques.

A good example of this conviction is the climate-controlled shopping center. After measuring populations, buying habits, incomes, and the like, the White Male System has built countless numbers of these malls throughout the country. You can spend hours in one without ever being aware of changes in temperature, humidity, or time of day. Shopping centers are only the beginning, though. Today, the local mall; tomorrow, the universe! The White Male System orients much of its research and development effort toward this goal of control. It has embraced the scientific method and distorted it until it has become a way to achieve godhood.

In its original secular form, the scientific method encouraged open-mindedness. It allowed a person the freedom to explore anything and gave her or him a process to use when doing so. One can see evidence of this by looking back at the lives of the great scientists. Since its adoption by the White Male System, however, the scientific method has undergone a significant change. It is now seen as the basis for supporting and proving the myths of the White Male System. It is no longer a tool of learning and exploration.

Many scientists and researchers today—especially those involved in the social sciences—use the scientific method to support their beliefs and biases. Many women and other minorities instinctively distrust the "findings" of the White Male System researcher, and for good cause. Often, these "findings" have little relation to fact. They are simply data which have been interpreted to suit the bias of the experimenter. They are then used to reinforce White Male System stereotypes and myths.

Part of this misuse of the scientific method involves an unquestioning faith in the validity of numbers. Numbers are essential to the scientific method, to which measurement is the key.

When we become convinced that numbers are real, though, we forget that they are only symbols that represent other realities. Numbers are just words in a foreign language. We can learn to speak French or

Spanish or Serbo-Croatian, and we can learn to speak numbers as well. But this does not mean that numbers have special powers.

Many people today suffer from what is commonly termed "math anxiety." In my work as a therapist, I have had several clients who simply could not do math. I became interested in this phenomenon and decided to find out more about it. After doing some research, I discovered that while none of my "math-anxious" clients had trouble with mathematics as a symbolic field, all had difficulty performing calculations.

In general, I found that people can be grouped into three categories with respect to math learning: 1. those who can not do math; 2. those who are able to perform calculations without any trouble; and 3. higher mathematicians and theoretical scientists. Interestingly, people who belong to group 1 not only have great difficulty performing calculations but also *do not believe in the reality of numbers or consider them very important* (although they will rarely verbalize this). Group 2 people—many of whom are high school or grade school math teachers, social scientists, CPA's, engineers, and other practical scientists—may *say* that numbers are not real but *they do not really mean it*. They act as if numbers are real because they truly think they are.

Psychologists are famous for this discrepancy between awareness and behavior. For example, they are taught that the IQ number has no real meaning, that it is only accurate within a relative range, and that it is basically an indicator, not a fact. But how many act as if they are really convinced of this? Not many! An IQ of 125 is always better than an IQ of 120, is it not?

Finally, group 3 people—and this usually includes artists and musicians as well as higher mathematicians and theoretical scientists—have no trouble using numbers or understanding that they are only a symbolic language. They accept the fact that numbers have limitations.

I have found that groups 1 and 3 can communicate with each other very nicely when they bypass group 2. Group 1 can understand math in much the same way as group 3 can—they simply are unable to perform calculations. They do very well with algebra, however. They can explore and utilize algebraic concepts, but they find numbers a distraction. Numbers get in the way of their ideas. This is usually because most group 1 persons have a sneaking (but accurate) suspicion that numbers are not real. It should come as no surprise that the majority of math-anxious people are women.

Our society is engulfed in numbers. Many of us feel as if we are sacrificing our own identity to them. We are lost without our social security numbers, credit card numbers, and telephone numbers, *ad nauseum*. Many more work hours are spent with numbers than they are in production or with people.

I once attended a church service in a small Midwestern town. Afterward, I told the minister how pleased I had been with the prayer and sermon meditation. He nodded and immediately launched into a discussion of church attendance and how few people were there on communion Sundays during summer. I had commented on the quality and content of the service—and he had responded with numbers!

The White Male System believes in the reality of numbers. It has to in order to support its own mythology. If numbers are not real—if they are merely symbols which are open to subjective interpretation—then they can not be used to measure, predict, and control.

Let me reiterate that I do not consider the White Male System all bad or the Female System (to be described later) all good. Each has its positive and negative points. Each can either help or hinder. The important thing to realize is that each is only a system.

Neither is the way the world is. We must learn to see this. When we do, we suddenly find that we have a wide range of choices where we originally thought none existed. And both power and wisdom are contained in the knowledge that one is free to choose.

I have explained the White Male System in terms of its myths and beliefs in order to establish a vocabulary for understanding. Once we acknowledge that the White Male System is no more than the sum of its parts—and that those parts are open to question—we can begin to change it. We can begin to see other realities as viable options and learn to trust ourselves again.

The Female System is one other reality. It exists in two forms. One is a reactive system that has been developed to cope with and stay safe within the White Male System. We must share our insights about ourselves and men from the reactive system we have established. If we do this we can begin to see a new Female System emerging when women become clear and trusting of our own perceptions.

# CHAPTER TWO

# THE ORIGINAL SIN OF BEING BORN FEMALE

## HOW WOMEN SEE THEMSELVES AND OTHER WOMEN

One of the first things I noticed when I began my intensive study of women is that we normally do not like or trust one another. This was evident in the comments I often heard prior to women's weekend workshops: "How am I going to survive a whole weekend surrounded by women?" "What on earth are we going to do during all that time?" "What are we going to find to talk about?" Other women got right to the point: "Well, I guess I can see spending a whole weekend with women, but how are we going to accomplish anything without male leaders?"

Since the women's movement has become more accepted and acceptable, this dislike and distrust of other women has become more subtle, but it is still there. The women who are most often subjected to it are those who emerge as the leaders of the movement. They are blamed for most of the problems women are experiencing today and are frequently verbally attacked, or "trashed."

In general, women feel relatively safe attacking other women. We are not dependent on each other for our identity, so what does it matter? This ongoing antipathy has severely hindered the growth and maturation of the Female System. The White Male System has used its observation of women inflicting pain on one another to discount the Female System.

When women say, "I do not like or trust other women," what we are really saying is, "I don't like myself." And this in turn can be expanded to "I don't like femaleness."

I have heard this expressed in group after group. A gifted commercial artist who was new to the women's movement once said, "This is all very fine, but I still think that deep, meaningful conversations can only happen with men." Other women have said, "I'm not like other women," or "My best and most interesting friends are men." One woman who was listening to a female announcer on the radio commented, "I really don't like women's voices."

In other words, what women were saying when we felt safe was that to be born female means to be born innately inferior, damaged, that there is something innately "wrong" with us.

Several years ago I was doing a weekend workshop with a group of competent and influential women. They were all successful and well-respected in their chosen fields. They appeared confident and self-assured and were obviously intelligent and skillful. As the weekend wore on, each woman began to reveal basic feelings of self-doubt. Each expressed a sense that deep down inside there was something seriously wrong with her. Each was convinced that she was not okay, that she had been born "tainted," that she was inadequate or not good enough or somehow worthless. And each tried to conceal these feelings by developing her own personal "coping mechanism."

One woman projected an image of "toughness." She walked with a strong, confident stride and carried herself assertively. She took on many tasks that the others would not have dared to try and always completed them. After an accident in which she cut herself seriously, she went to the hospital, got stitches, and returned to complete the workshop.

She had been the only woman on a university counseling center staff for many years. Her position was not tenured and she did not have her Ph.D., yet the students consistently rated her the best supervisor. She was a survivor and good at it. During the workshop, she managed to convince me that going through the Grand Canyon on a raft could be fun (which it was!) and that sitting up front "where the action is" was the only way to run the rapids (which it was not!).

Almost everyone in the group admired and cared for this woman and frequently looked to her as a model of success. She had "arrived." Nevertheless, as she began to focus on herself and on personal issues, it became clear that she "knew" there was something wrong with her. She felt that she had to be tough or people would take advantage of her. She believed that one had to be prepared for anything or end up with nothing. Although she appeared strong and self-confident to those around her, she held her sadness inside and was uneasy in asking for support. Hard on the outside, she was really gentle and vulnerable. Much of her attitude of toughness was developed to cope with deep feelings of inadequacy.

Another woman in the group was a scholar. She was an outstanding graduate student, consistently made A's on her examinations and papers, and was thought to have an exceptionally fine mind. Although she had not yet completed her doctorate, she had already received several excellent job offers. Everyone respected her and looked up to her. Yet the more she opened herself to the group, the more apparent it became that she was terrified of failure. Nothing she did was ever "good enough." If only she had tried harder, she could have done better! If only she had taken more time or studied more, she could have come further! She had convinced herself that nothing but perfection in everything she did could counter her fundamental imperfection of being born female.

Another woman in the group was very beautiful. Her hair, clothing, and makeup were always impeccable. She was chic and attractive. Some of the women had known her before the workshop and said she was always the center of attention at cocktail parties, especially among the men. The other women in the group envied her and some even hated her! She was always getting the male validation and approval that they sought, and they perceived that she took it away from them because they believed that there was never enough to go around.

The more this woman worked with the group, the clearer it became that she, too, felt worthless and insecure. She knew that men were attracted to her because she was gorgeous and seductive, but she had no proof that they really *liked* her. What would happen when she "faded?"

She began to reveal other deep-seated anxieties. Had her husband married her because he loved and respected her, or because she had gone to bed with him before they were married? Did he genuinely like and value her or was she simply an ornament to him?

She did not value herself. Without male validation and approval, she was sure she would have nothing. Like the other women in the group, she felt that there was something intrinsically wrong with her. As she revealed her inner feelings, the group warmed to her and became more accepting of her.

And so it went. One woman after another shed her appearance of confidence and high self-esteem, revealing that down deep she *knew* there was something wrong with her. Each acknowledged that much of her behavior was to compensate for her "innate inferiority" and to hide it from herself and others.

As I worked with these women and watched them work with one another, I suddenly became aware that I was witnessing attempts to cope with the Original Sin of Being Born Female. To be born female in this culture means that you are born "tainted," that there is something intrinsically wrong with you that you can never change, that your birthright is one of innate inferiority. I am not implying that this must remain so. I do believe that we must know this and understand it as a given before it can be worked through and put to rest.

Male therapists, and men in general, have difficulty understanding what it means to be born with a birthright of innate inferiority. Men, of course, do struggle with feelings of inferiority and low self-esteem, but their feelings are because of an inability to be always superior. They cannot understand how deeply the feelings of innate inferiority penetrate our being and how ever-present they are. Regardless of how confident or competent a woman is, she struggles with this "given" in life.

I am reminded once again of what many white liberals experienced during the Black revolution. We were sure that we knew what it meant to be discriminated against. We thought that we could empathize with what our Black friends were going through. In truth, though, we could not. We could never really know what it was like to grow up Black in a white culture. The same is true of growing up female.

According to the theological concept of original sin, there is no real justification by works. Women can never absolve themselves of their Original Sin of Being Born Female. There is no "right thing" we can do to atone for it even though we spend much of our time and creative energy trying to.

# HOW WOMEN COPE WITH THE ORIGINAL SIN OF BEING BORN FEMALE

Over the years, women have developed a number of strategies for coping with their assigned inferiority. Several of them are ingenious though none works.

For instance, most women develop an unbelievable capacity to remember details of events. If a couple has a quarrel, it is usually the woman who will remember what she said, what he said, the sequence of events, the setting, and how each seemed to be feeling at any point in the argument. Men often turn to their partners to find out what they themselves said, when they said it, and how they phrased something in particular. They trust the women to remember the details—and the women almost always do!

I used to believe that women developed this skill just so they could be right *about* the facts of an issue or the circumstances of an event. Over time, I came to realize that it was far more complicated than that. Situations that were merely a question of the facts for men took on the proportions of a life-death struggle for the women. Sometimes it seemed as if they were fighting for their very souls! And they were!

Because women have worked so hard to develop memories for details, we can often prove ourselves right about any event or circumstance. Unfortunately, this only serves as a tension release. The issue of who is right and who is wrong is only a coverup for a deeper, more serious issue—that of being an innate "wrong."

True, we may "win" an argument because our memories help us to prove that we are right about specifics, but we do not feel any better afterward. We can never prove that we *ourselves* are "a right." For as long as we remain female, we are always "a wrong."

Some women use goodness as a strategy for absolution. We become very good. We overwhelm ourselves and those around us with our unquestionable goodness. We are so "good" that others become irritated with us and choose to avoid us altogether! Somehow, we believe that if we are just good enough, we will be absolved of our Original Sin of Being Born Female. It never works. Others take advantage of our goodness but that never relieves our internal feelings of unease and wrongness.

Some women embrace fairness as a strategy. Women are noted for fairness. We strive to be fair even at our own expense. We are careful to evaluate persons we meet and situations in which we find ourselves in terms of fairness. People tell us that we complain too much about the injustice in the world. I believe that this is because we wholeheartedly believe in an ultimate fairness. It must be there—all we have to do is find it!

Most women believe this fairness exists in the legal system. Despite clear evidence to the contrary, we keep trusting that the legal system is a system of justice. We forget that laws are made by the White Male System to promulgate its values and support its myths. Many of us collide with the White Male System's law in the divorce courts. Women go into the divorce court, telling the judge the truth and expecting the judge to be fair. Often they suffer financially and emotionally and are stripped of their last hope for ultimate fairness.

I have a friend who is a judge, and she once said to me, "Sometimes I just cannot be fair. I have to go by the law and I can try to interpret it with leniency, but where the law is unfair I cannot be fair."

Women are not the only victims of this naivete. As I was driving through New Mexico some years ago, I picked up a man who was having car trouble. He told me that he was from an old Spanish land-grant family and was studying the law. There was a great deal of confusion at that time about land ownership in New Mexico, and he was determined to do something about it. He and several other families were planning to take their case to the Supreme Court.

Long before New Mexico became a state, the United States had made a treaty with Spain regarding the land under question. The man was confident that the Supreme Court would understand and respect this. How could the United States refuse to honor such an important treaty? Would that not be internationally embarrassing? With great confidence, he stated that he and his colleagues were going to tell the Court the truth, and it could not help but see who really owned the land. I asked him whether he had talked with any Native Americans lately!

The legal system is a game, and white men know how to play it to win. After all, they made the rules!

Several years ago, one of my clients was stopped by a patrolman for no apparent reason on the way home from a political rally. The party sticker on her car differed from the political preference of most of the police in the city, and in her neighborhood (which was unusual in its racial and political mix) there had been several reports of police harassment which the residents connected to the campaign. My client was angry about being stopped and demanded to know why before she would show her driver's license. Words and a scuffle ensued and she was dragged, hand-cuffed, to the police station where she was put in a cell. By this time, she was so incensed that she took off her shoe, ran it back and forth across the bars, and spewed out a verbal harangue. She was told that she was not acting like a white woman (she was very white, middle class), and her response was, "Yes, I am. White women are angry, too!" All in all, she had quite a night of it. She was booked on several charges and was forced to encounter the legal system. While her feminist ideals dictated that she retain a feminist woman as her lawyer, she also wanted to win. So instead she selected a very shrewd, male lawyer who had a reputation for winning. He was not someone she would probably have chosen as a personal friend.

She was nervous when they went to court. Her lawyer assured her that everything would be all right even though it appeared as if the D.A. and police were "out to get her." He arrived in court with what looked like a rather large suitcase. When she asked what it was, he said that it was his "courtroom briefcase." He explained that it was his secret psychological weapon. He would stuff it with briefs, law books, manila folders, papers, etc. Then he would drag it into the courtroom (a good showman) and spread its contents out on the table. He said that he had usually won his case by this time. He did! She did! Most of the charges were dropped and a minor charge with a low fine was agreed upon. It so happened that justice was served. Not because of justice, but because her lawyer played the game and played it to win.

Fairness is important for individual and system integrity. Women's fairness is regularly exploited. It is used to keep us down and maintain our lower position in society. No matter how fair we are, we can never absolve ourselves of our Original Sin of Being Born Female.

Along similar lines, some women cope with being female in the White Male System by following the rules. We learn them and carefully follow them in the hope of becoming like everyone else and blending in. Unfortunately, we are always disappointed.

Whenever I do organizational consulting, I look to the women and the minorities in the group to tell me about the procedures of their organization. I am constantly impressed with how well they know them. This does not seem to matter, though. Time and again, I hear women and minorities voicing two complaints: As soon as they develop some expertise in their organization's rules, someone changes them! Or, once they have the rules down pat, they observe that the men stop following them. Because white men make the rules, they assume the right to modify or even break them.

Other women attempt to seek absolution for the Original Sin of Being Born Female by developing an incredible capacity for being understanding. Although both men and women believe that men know and understand everything, we constantly try to *be* understanding. This fits well with our attention to details. We constantly gather information on almost everything, especially anything that has to do with relationships. But the need to understand goes far deeper than mere curiosity. We understand why this or that happened, and *we forgive.*

*Men* are supposed to be the ones who know and understand everything. Yet most men will say that they feel best understood by women and look to them for true understanding!

I was fascinated with this phenomenon, because it seems to contradict the mythology of the White Male System, so I began to look at the word *understand.* If one stands under, one had better understand that those who stand over have the power and the influence. If one over-stands, then one does not have to understand. Understanding is for the under-standers. Over-standing is a secure position. Curious, is it not?

What has resulted from all of women's coping strategies? Have our excellent memories, or goodness, or fairness, or conformity to the rules, or understanding ever really accomplished anything? Not really. As in the theological concept of original sin there is no justification by works. However, we are told that we can turn to an outside intermediary for help. We can look to someone else to intercede for us. We are taught that once we attach ourselves to a male, we can get validation and approval. In this way, we will feel better

and be absolved of our Original Sin of Being Born
Female. Unfortunately, this usually does not work
either, and we continue to struggle with intense feelings
of worthlessness.

## LOOKING BACK AT THE "OLD BOYS": MEN'S TRADITIONAL INTERPRETATION OF WOMEN

As I became more and more interested in women's
psychology, I frequently went back to reread some of the
"old boys" in the field—Sigmund Freud and Erik
Erikson in particular. Many of them were very astute
observers and deserve to be recognized as such. Few of
them were good interpreters of women, however. They
could gather data, but they could not analyze and
evaluate it objectively. Their interpretations of their
observations were almost always incorrect because they
could only interpret from their own, White Male
System, bias.

Freud observed that women envy men, and that
was an excellent observation. But *why* do women envy
men? Because, said Freud, they do not have something
men have—namely, a penis. Freud's penis was extremely
important to him. So when he observed that women
envy men, he assumed that women envied what he
valued most.

I have met very few women who really wish they
had a penis. In general, women prefer that penises stay
right where they are—attached to men. There is
something men have that we would very much like to
have though: the birthright of innate superiority, the
power and influence one inherits by being born male. A
man can be less competent or knowledgeable than a
woman, but he still has the advantage over her simply
because he is a man. It really does not matter whether

or not men consciously know that they have this
birthright. Most assume it at a very basic level. Women
know it and this awareness affects the way we see
ourselves, men and other women.

Erikson was a keen observer and a brilliant
conceptualizer. He noted that female children and
females, in general, seemed to feel an inner space, or
emptiness and that their psychological orientation was
related to this inner space. That was a good observation.
Like Freud, however, Erikson interpreted his data from
his cultural male bias.

Erikson decided that this inner space was located in
the lower abdomen and was related to the female's
identity. He believed that the vagina and the uterus
remained empty until it was filled by a penis (in other
words, until the female attached herself to a male) and
then a baby. At that point, the woman secured her
identity and became whole.

Women *do* experience an inner space. We never
describe it as being in the lower abdomen, however. It is
almost always in the solar plexus. Women use various
words and phrases to name it—hole, pit, nothingness,
void, "black" space, cavern. We are fearful of it and
vulnerable to it. In strange, unfamiliar, or threatening
situations, we will often stand with our arms folded over
our solar plexus—our *cavern*. Women have also
developed body postures that "sink in" and protect this
area. We often cover it with fat.

Our cavern is central to our identity and
wholeness, but it has nothing to do with penises and
babies. Instead, it is related to the fact that we go from
being our fathers' daughters to being our husbands'
wives and finally our sons' mothers. It is related to our
Original Sin of Being Born Female and our need to look
outside ourselves for validation and approval. When we
begin to determine who we are from inside, our cavern
begins to get smaller.

A woman's cavern is where she houses her Original Sin of Being Born Female. We are always aware of it and the need to shrink and fill it. I believe that this is one reason why so many women have eating and drinking problems.

I have observed many women in therapy sessions either putting their hands over this area or bending over to protect it. As a woman begins to establish her own internal identity, her cavern begins to shrink and heal, but it can very easily be torn open again. This happens most frequently when a woman is faced with ending a primary relationship with a man that has given her validation and approval. It also happens when things in general start going wrong in a woman's life. Many women describe this feeling as similar to going over the top on a roller-coaster ride. Suddenly, terrifyingly, the bottom drops out!

I once lectured at a well-known Eastern university where the women in the audience were very taken with the "cavern" theory. They agreed that it was real and true for them, and then one of them said, "Okay, I agree that I have a cavern. Now tell me how to get rid of it and how to keep it gone!" I answered that this cavern is integral to the experience of being female in our culture and that I had never met anyone who had completely rid herself of it. Many women do establish an internal identity, feel "full," and have little or no experience of their cavern for long periods of time. Let something major go wrong in their lives, though, and they are immediately aware of it again. The cavern may not be as large or the feeling of emptiness as intense as before, but it is still there inside their solar plexus.

There was a woman in one of my groups who was constantly in Weight Watchers. Even during a therapy session, she would nibble away on celery and carrot sticks. After she had participated in the group for some time and was clearly on her way toward becoming her own person, she began to change. One night she made a surprising announcement: She was getting full. She seemed to be filling up from the inside. She was not hungry anymore! The other members of the group smiled knowingly. They knew her and knew what she was feeling. They had watched her reclaim her identity.

A nun in one of my workshops had been doing some very deep process work in relation to her cavern—or "hole" as she preferred to call it. Near the end of the workshop, she came up with this play on words: "My hole is my wholeness. My wholeness is my hole. Without my hole, I would not have my wholeness." Because of her, I reached a new level of understanding. I began to realize that women's caverns contain the essence of being female in a White Male System. Unless we recognize this and accept it, we cannot grow. To establish an identity is only a part of the growth process. We must understand the forces that are working against this process both within us and without.

Whenever I got too far off the track with my Black friends, they used to tell me, "Don't take away my Blackness! That is who I *am!*" To be Black in a White Male System results in certain experiences. To be female in a White Male System results in certain experiences. Recognizing this fact is part of the process of knowing and accepting who we are.

Many women feel that they cannot be whole without a man. We look to men to provide us with wholeness and fill our cavern. When this fails, we blame ourselves and feel even worse. Some women prefer the status of being divorced to that of being single. To them, having had a man at one time is better than never having had one.

Women are often terrified of being alone. Being "connected" to someone else—a man—ensures their survival. They do not understand that even when no

one else is around they are still with someone—
themselves.

Remember that in the Original Sin concept, we can
only be "saved" with the help and intervention of an
outside intermediary. We are taught that we will be all
right if we can only attach ourselves to an innately
superior being, a man, who will then intercede for us.
We will feel good again. We will be absolved of being
born female. What this means, of course, is that we see
other women as competitors for the "goodies"—male
validation and approval. Men also participate in this
thinking by setting up a situation that suggests "You
and her fight—over me and for my attention."

Women often complain—and rightfully—that we are
only sex objects. We do not like it when men are
interested only in our bodies. We find it insulting, and it
angers us. What we fail to see is that the culture is
equally destructive to men in setting them up as
marriage objects. Because we believe we need to be
attached to a male so that he can absolve us of our
Original Sin of Being Born Female, we try very hard to
"get one." Women often do not even need to know the
men we marry. Perhaps, some feel, it is better that we do
not know them! I have known some women who cling
to the state of marriage even when the husband lives
elsewhere and gives no financial or emotional support. Is
this any less destructive than using another person as a
sex object? *Too often, men and women objectify each other.*

Many women work hard to do all the "right"
things. They find nice men, attach themselves, produce
lovely children (male children are especially important),
devote themselves to homemaking, and still feel
unhappy. Then they assume that they are at fault. "I
have done everything this culture has told me to do,"
their unconscious tells them, "but still I have not been
absolved of my Original Sin of Being Born Female.
There must be something wrong with me!" Few

question the culture that tells women they will feel better if and only if they are saved by male validation and approval.

Many of us unknowingly play one of the most deadly yet popular male-female games. We put men on pedestals because we need them to absolve us. At the same time, we resent their being there and chip away at their pedestals, doing whatever we can to prove to them and ourselves that they are only human and not at all superior. Then, when they fall off their pedestals, we panic! If men are really not superior, who can provide our absolution?

At this point the game gets even more complicated. Once we have seen men off the pedestal, we set about trying to put them back again. Some of us rush to embrace the White Male System and its definition of a woman's role in relation to a man. We become Total Women. We help the men back to their pedestals, only to resent their being up again. Most men are not aware of this process while it is happening. They only know that something is not right. In therapy sessions, some men have described this feeling in terms of riding an elevator. They have the internal experience of going up and down again and again without understanding why, and their relationships deteriorate into mutual dishonesty and manipulation.

Many women simply do not know how to live without playing these destructive games. Since we grow up in a foreign culture—a White Male System which is always defined as "right"—we tend not to trust our own perceptions unless they are consonant with those of the White Male System. Whenever we have different perceptions—whenever we try to explore other realities—we are told that we are sick, bad, crazy, stupid, ugly, or incompetent. And whenever we receive that message from those around us, we grab our solar plexus and run!

I have yet to meet a woman who has not
acknowledged her own particular fear—of being sick,
bad, crazy, stupid, etc.—and embraced it. We do this
rather than heeding our own healthy perceptions. When
someone implies that we are "really off the wall" or "just
do not understand how things are," most of us, unless
we have successfully confronted our caverns, will back
off from our own perceptions and busily demonstrate
how we see things just the way everyone else does.
Frequently, women deny the way we see the world or
the values we have in order to gain male validation and
approval. We resist seeing that what is happening to us
is happening because we are female. Instead, we blame
our unhappiness and lack of fulfillment on some "flaw"
in our character. We try to believe that we are not
understanding enough, or we are not smart enough, or
we are not pretty or witty or good enough. Some of us
develop life-long excuses to explain and interpret our
experience.

For many years, my favorite excuse for myself was
my "obnoxious personality." I once worked as a clinical
director in a state mental health facility where I
frequently was expected to present what I felt were
sound ideas to the men on the staff. I would try to
present them in a straightforward fashion and was
puzzled when my ideas were quietly ignored at the time
but eagerly approved when they were put forth by men
soon after. I used to wonder why no one paid any
attention to me—until I decided that it must be due to
my "obnoxious personality." If only I were not so
abrasive.

I had these thoughts before I became involved in
the women's movement. Then, not long after I began
learning about women's issues, I realized what I had
been doing to myself. I started trying to filter out how
much of my lack of success was due to my self-
proclaimed "obnoxious personality" and how much was

due to the fact that I was a female in a White Male System. I learned that about 90 percent of what was happening to me at work and in my life was because I was female in a White Male System, not because I was obnoxious. I was simply getting my cultural due.

We have all developed our own pet excuses for what has happened to us during our lives. Some are quite ingenious: "Maybe they aren't listening to me because my legs are too fat!"

No wonder we feel different! No wonder we feel estranged from ourselves and other women. From childhood we are told that we do not belong, that we can never be included in the "in" group. We are always on the outside looking in. Often we believe that other women have "made it" and we are the only ones who have not. I have heard many women hesitantly express their feelings of alienation in women's groups, convinced that they are the only ones who feel alone. They are surprised when the other members of the group acknowledge identical feelings. We have become isolated from one another, and this has blinded us to the commonality of our experience.

Because our position in this culture is so shaky, we have learned to lie. We lie to men and to other women, but mostly we lie to ourselves. We lie about who we are and about what we want and need. By learning to lie, we feel that we can carve out a niche for ourselves, but what this really does is to intensify our isolation and sense of not belonging. Once we start being honest with ourselves and with other women, though, our feelings of isolation lessen. Our cavern begins to shrink and fill up.

Women frequently go along with the expectations of the White Male System in order to win acceptance. Most of us do this in one of two ways: we either try to act out the White Male System's definition of the traditional "proper" woman, or we try to be "like men." The latter choice is especially common among professional women. I can remember a time when the nicest compliment I thought I could ever get was that I thought like a man. Of course I thought like a man! I was very well trained in the White Male System, but could men think like women?

Many women believe that the only road to success is to act like men and beat them at their own game. Some women embrace the tenets of the White Male System more avidly than men themselves do. This tactic can be self-defeating, however. If women are too successful, they are punished. We try to be intelligent—but our intelligence must never threaten men. We try to be competent—but our competence must never overshadow that of men.

Some people believe that the women's movement has changed the inequality between the sexes, but they are mistaken. Perhaps men can no longer tell us directly that we cannot be intelligent or competent or successful, but they can certainly imply it in subtle ways. If we can not behave like "real" women, then we had better become adept at behaving like men! Whole industries have sprung up that purport to teach women how to succeed in business. The major underlying message of these programs is nothing more than a variation on the theme of "why can't a woman be more like a man?" So we try. We try very hard. We dress in tailored suits and are careful not to wear anything that draws attention to our breasts. We carry briefcases and learn to assert ourselves. Then we come face to face with the old Catch-22: "We are equal, but some are more equal than others." We must conform to White Male System values and procedures, but we must never threaten the men with or for whom we work.

Somewhere along the line, women have also become convinced that all successful men "go it alone." (They ignore the existence of "old boys" groups and mentors.) So they determine that they will go it alone, too. I call this the "Invictus" myth ("My head is bloody, but unbowed!"). We start believing that it is somehow dishonorable to build support groups or ask for help. When we turn to others for assistance or support, we are only admitting our weakness—and no man would ever do that! What good would it do to ask a woman for help anyway?

Many women take this attitude one step further. Since we are trained to dislike and distrust one another, we often find it difficult to support one another's efforts. We do not stop there. We actively set about trying to destroy our competition. Some believe that there is not enough room at the top for too many successful women, so others of us will just have to be kicked down the ladder again (or never let up at all).

If one's validation and sense of worth come from "not being like other (inferior) women," then it is critical to be one of the few who succeed in the superior male world. I like to call this push to succeed the "Queen Bee" syndrome. It accounts in part for the phenomenon of successful "token" women dissociating themselves from the women's movement. We refuse to give credit to the women who have gone before us and made it possible for us to have higher paying jobs or get tenure or become Managerial Women. "I made it on my merits alone, and so can you!" "What are you complaining about? All you have to do is try!" What is implied here is the old saw that "if you were not inferior, you'd be successful too."

Women who buy into the White Male System often use power—when they get it—like men: against other women and to destroy them. Our dislike and distrust of femaleness goes very deep.

## DEALING WITH RAGE

It is no secret that women in general are very, very

angry. Nobody likes to be innately inferior. Blacks do not like it. Chicanos do not like it. Women do not like it.

I mentioned earlier how important fairness is to women. We need to believe that the White Male System is fair or we have no hope at all. Of course, it is not at all fair to be defined as "inferior" at birth because of one's sex. This is one of the major sources of women's rage.

Related to this—and producing concommitant rage—is the cultural myth that if a woman does all the right things, is good, and suffers, she will be happy. Unfortunately, even if we do everything our culture tells us to do, we still feel awful! We fold our arms over our solar plexus and groan.

In the early stages of identifying and dealing with their rage, many women direct the blame toward their mothers. "Why didn't she tell me? She must have known what would happen to me. Why did she keep it from me?" We have been duped!

Somewhere along the line, most women make the startling discovery that the superior male beings who are supposed to save us from the Original Sin of Being Born Female are not superior at all. They are just ordinary folks. We have been duped again! Men cannot even take care of themselves—how can we trust them to take care of us? Where can we turn if they can not absolve us or intercede for us? Men's humanness frightens us and we hate them for it.

Some women never acknowledge this. They tell themselves that the perfect man must be out there somewhere. If only they can find him! They rid themselves of their husbands and go in search of "real" men. A woman may try several relationships and marriages before she understands that the pursuit of the innately superior male is a disappointing quest. Many men try to fulfill that image of superiority but, happily, remain quite human.

We may then begin to question the culture that taught us that attaching ourselves to a male absolves us of our Original Sin of Being Born Female. This becomes another source of rage.

The question, then, is not whether women are angry, but what we do with our anger. In my work with women, I have found that we channel our rage in several ways.

First, there is the super-competent woman. By being the best at whatever it is that she decides to do, she accomplishes two things: she overcomes her innately inferior position, and she sets herself above those around her. She uses her competence as a weapon. She no longer feels that she has to have anything to do with other women. She has made it, so she has no use for or interest in women's liberation. In her opinion, women are not held down—isn't she proof of that? She pulled herself up on her own—let other women help themselves! More often than not, she is a veritable taskmaster (I use that word intentionally.) She drives herself and everybody else, thinking that she can vent her rage by exercising her power over others. Both men and women end up despising her.

Then there is the seductress. She is unusually pretty, works hard to keep her good figure, and always dresses beautifully. She uses her sexuality to attract men and compete with women. Her power comes from the knowledge that she can have sexual control over men, and she often uses it with satisfaction and cruelty. What can be more satisfying than getting a penis to rise—and then doing nothing about it?

Or there is the ultrafeminine woman. She is very passive and inert and always defers to men because they are wiser and stronger. She does everything she can to protect the fragile male ego. Her weakness is her power, and she uses it to make men completely dependent on her for reassurances of their maleness. Men become her captives and cannot function without her (she sees to that!).

Or there is the chemically dependent or overweight woman. She vents her anger by abusing herself and her body. She also punishes those around her with her erratic and self-destructive behavior. Her anger seems passive, but she uses it effectively to control her world.

There is also the depressed woman. Depression in women almost always goes hand in hand with rage turned against the self. The depressed woman suffers, and she has learned to use her depression as a weapon, making sure those around her suffer as well. Unfortunately, she is often destroyed in the process.

The neighborhood gossip expresses her rage by talking maliciously about other women—but rarely about men. By attacking almost everyone else around her, she believes that she can win male approval.

Finally, there is the "Good Christian Martyr." This embodiment of anger is generally supported by our culture—especially by the church. The Good Christian Martyr releases her rage through sacrifice and suffering. She always takes the smallest piece of meat at mealtime. If there is not enough dessert to go around, she does without. She never buys any clothes for herself because she is not important, but she always makes sure that her children and her husband have new clothes. She gains control over others by inducing guilt. She is perhaps the most manipulative and powerful of all angry women. Some of the most damaged women I have worked with in therapy are those who have had Good Christian Martyr mothers. They try but they can never live up to the image of their perfect mothers who sacrificed so much.

Each of these women lets anger run her life. She cannot fight the White Male System, she can never atone for her Original Sin of Being Born Female, but she can turn her anger into a weapon. However, because women are angry and show this in different ways does not mean that they are purposefully evil or bad. They are simply doing their best to cope with a culture which labels them as innately inferior and denies any direct or healthy outlet for the anger that results from the inequity or their position.

The societal belief in the Original Sin of Being Born Female has created women's distrust of power in themselves and in other women. We also fear our use of power because it so readily combines with our unexpressed rage and becomes terrifying to ourselves and those around us.

What results from all of this is the creation of a vicious cycle. We direct our rage toward our partners and our children, and they in turn become angry with us—which only makes us angrier!

## WOMEN'S SEXUAL SELVES

A major casualty of the Original Sin of Being Born Female is misunderstood sexuality. We find our sexuality very difficult to cope with, both internally and externally. I believe that women in general know very little about female sexuality because men have always been the ones to define it. I know few women who have been able to define for themselves what their sexuality means to them.

This is probably the best example of what happens when we learn to fear and distrust our own perceptions and label them as sick, bad, crazy, stupid, and so on. Since sex has traditionally been considered men's prerogative, and since men are supposed to know and understand everything, women let them set the ground rules. We let men tell us how we are supposed to feel, behave, and respond. We let them dictate how we should experience our innermost selves.

I have made several observations about women's sexuality. I realize—and emphasize here—that these are only observations and do not constitute the last word on or even a clear picture of female sexuality.

First, we do not categorize individuals and situations according to their sexuality. Second, we do not assume that each and every relationship must be sexual, nor do we view everything we do and everyone we meet as having some sexual significance. In fact, women do not define the world in sexual terms.

Unfortunately, this is seen as contrary to the way the White Male System experiences and defines the world. So we are told, once again—both directly and indirectly—that we are wrong. When we refuse to categorize all persons and relationships as having sexual meaning for us, we are informed that we are frigid or afraid of sex. That *we* have a problem.

Historically, women have been defined (by men) as being sexually pure and pristine. The only perfect woman was a detached and innocent virgin. "Nice women" did not enjoy sex. There were good women, and there were whores. This theory was most prevalent during the late 1800's and early 1900's, but it continues today. Many men still categorize women as either nice or whorish. Pity the woman who is sexually responsive or assertive to a man—even if he is her husband!

The onset of the sexual revolution meant that men needed to change this definition. Suddenly, "sexually liberated" women were expected to act like "sexually liberated" men wanted them to—in other words, they were supposed to sleep around. No one bothered to ask women what we thought sexual liberation involved.

I have found that most women do not attribute the same degree of importance to sex that men do. In particular, we rarely want—or are comfortable with—multiple sexual relationships. We may have a number of sexual partners on the way to establishing our own sexual identity, but we are usually more comfortable expressing our sexual selves with one other person. Most women feel that it is difficult to focus their attention and sexual energy with more than one person at a time. This directly relates to the fact that, for many women, sex is one and *only* one aspect of the totality of intimacy and lovemaking. Lovemaking involves the whole being and is a completely different experience from simply having sex.

I am very interested in what has been touted as the "cult of the orgasm." Both men and women have fallen victim to it. If one does not have an orgasm, then something is wrong. If one does not "give" one's partner an orgasm, then something is wrong. And who should have an orgasm first? Should both partners have theirs at the same time?

According to what women have told me, they do not put the same value on the orgasm as men do. Intercourse and orgasms are far less important than touching, holding, stroking, and cuddling. Many women have reported that they participate in sex because of the touching and holding involved and do not consider intercourse the ultimate goal. They see sex as a medium for contact and closeness. Women's sexuality seems more intimately connected to relationships than mens', and sex for women can be difficult or even unpleasant outside the context of a meaningful relationship.

This is due in some degree to the fact that women intensely dislike being used as sex objects. Several women have told me that the only way they can deal with the discrepancies between their intellectual, emotional, and sexual (that is, sex-object) selves is by disassociating themselves from their bodies. Intelligent women who also happen to be beautiful are especially apt to do this. They are able to accept themselves as attractive sex objects at some level, but they place more value on their sensitivity and intellectual capacity. So they stop being aware of themselves from the neck down. They still dress their bodies to attract men, but they are not really "present" in their bodies. These women frequently report that they experience little or no sensation during sex but "fake it" in order to get male validation and approval.

I have worked closely with many of these women, trying to get their heads and bodies back in touch with each other. There was one woman who particularly moved me. A "Southern belle," she was an intelligent and competent person. She was also strikingly beautiful. During her therapy sessions, I would frequently ask her what she was feeling—and she never knew. Once, when I asked that question during a group meeting, tears started rolling down her cheeks. She confessed that she never felt anything below the neck! As she explored this further, she realized that it had begun when she was in high school. She had not been able to find a way to reconcile her intelligence with her beauty and was afraid of being a sex object, so she had resolved the problem by sacrificing her feelings. Whatever happened to her body from that point on—or whatever her body did or did not do—had nothing to do with who she really was.

Somehow sexuality has been invested with more meaning and importance than any other human characteristic. Sex can confirm or deny love. It can confirm or deny one's validity and worth as a woman or a man. It can confirm or deny the seriousness of a commitment. It can be the only acceptable source of nurturing and caring. It can also, of course, be a form of power wielded by one person over another.

Very little sexual activity goes on in our culture that is not overloaded with surplus psychological baggage. We do not have sex just for the sheer pleasure of making love; we do not have sex for the simple purpose of making babies. Instead, many of us are looking for the love and affirmation we never got from our angry mothers. We are asking another person to tell us that we are okay. We are handing ourselves over, but we are looking for something to be handed back in return. That something is often far more than the other person can ever give.

A woman's cavern may not be the center of her sexuality, as Erikson mistakenly assumed, but it is often at the center of how we feel about ourselves as sexual beings. If we carry years of rage and the Original Sin of Being Born Female within us, it will stand in the way of how we relate to ourselves and to others. We will either learn to use our sexuality as a weapon, fake it, or pretend it does not exist.

# CHAPTER THREE

# GETTING ALONG: MALE/FEMALE RELATIONSHIPS IN THE WHITE MALE SYSTEM

## HOW WOMEN SEE MEN

Most women have a pretty good idea of how men see them, but they are reluctant to verbalize their own ideas on how they see men. This happens for two reasons. First, we frequently distrust our own perceptions, and this makes us hesitant to express them. And second, when we do express them and they are different from the way men see things, we are dismissed and ridiculed.

Nevertheless, we cannot help but form opinions of men, even though we must often keep them to ourselves. Some of these opinions are given us by the White Male System and others stem from our own observations and experiences.

I have already said that women are taught from birth that men are innately superior. As a result, we expect and hope that they will be. We may know inside that they are not, but we try to ignore this because we believe that we need them to absolve us of our Original Sin of Being Born Female. We want them to save us from our birthright of inferiority. Some men do their best to live up to our expectations, but they cannot help wondering what, or who, they are supposed to save us from, and why!

We look to men to be superior while simultaneously

resenting and hating their birthright. We place men on pedestals, and this, needless to say, makes relaxed, caring relationships almost impossible. We cannot really relate to someone above us. We do our best to "catch a husband"—and far too frequently discover that we have not caught what we thought.

Women also need to see men as all-knowing and all-understanding. Many women feel misunderstood most of the time (as well they might!) and spend much of their lives seeking understanding. When we do not feel as if the men in our lives understand us, we blame ourselves for not communicating properly. We struggle desperately not to accept the awareness that men do not understand us completely because they cannot. They are able to understand little—if anything—beyond the pale of the White Male System unless they take special care to because they do not believe other systems exist.

It takes a great deal of strength, patience, and caring for an "inferior" person to teach his or her system to a "superior" person. It also takes about twice as much energy as communicating with a peer does. This is because "superior" system people are often slow learners and are not very motivated to learn about other systems. Why should they? They're already in charge! The Blacks learned this when they tried to communicate their system to the whites; many of them decided that it wasn't worth the effort.

Since men have been brainwashed—by their own system and by women—into thinking that they are superior and that they know and understand everything, they assume that they can tell us who we are and what we are like. Not only do they assume that they have the *right* to tell us who we are but also that they are *correct* in their perceptions of us and that we will accept whatever they say. We resent this very much! We want men to say, "Tell me what you are like;" instead we hear them saying, "Let *me* tell you what you are like!" Whenever we try to explain the Female System to them, they reply, "Put this information into the language and concepts of *my* system so I can understand it." It is almost as if they are saying, "It's *your* responsibility to make me understand. If I don't understand, it's *your* fault. It's not up to me to learn another system!"

I used to think that it was my sacred duty to help every man "understand" the Female System. I now have a new policy: I explain the concepts I'm trying to get across twice. If men do not appear as if they are beginning to understand what I am saying by then, I tell them that *they* have a problem!

Of course confronting them like this goes against another important fact that women are expected to know about men: namely, that their egos are very fragile *codependence* and need to be "protected." Many women devote their entire lives to caring for the "fragile male ego."

They believe the myth that men cannot tolerate the knowledge that they are not always good lovers, that they do not know and understand everything, that they are not always strong, that they do not always have to be "in charge"—in other words, that they are human like the rest of us. However, by believing and fostering the myth that men have fragile egos which need protecting, women assure themselves of being indispensable. If we are the only ones who can protect their egos, then how can they live without us?

It is important to look at whom we choose to protect. We *usually* protect those whom we see as weaker and more vulnerable than ourselves. In addition to assuring us a place of indispensability, this results in keeping the protected person weak and vulnerable. Thus, the cycle continues.

Some women have been willing to be honest and risk their position of indispensability with the men in their lives. They have found that men can, indeed,

tolerate the knowledge that they are not always good
lovers; they can tolerate knowing that they are only
human; they can tolerate knowing any number of things
when that information is presented in a caring way and
not as a weapon of resentment against a "superior"
being. They may not like the information but they can
tolerate it. This process, in turn, opens the door for
more honest and mutually satisfying relationships.

A woman once told me, "Oh sure, I know all this,
but I hide what I know from my husband. I protect him
so he is able to get out front and do the dirty work.
What woman in her right mind would want to fool
around with finances, economics, and politics?" Yet
when men take charge of these areas, we have to live
with their decisions whether or not we like them. More
and more of us are becoming less willing to do this.

There is another aspect of the male ego that is
important. Anyone who ever takes an elementary
biology course learns about one-celled organisms called
amoebas. The amoeba can assume any shape, and its
main goal in life is food-gathering. Whenever it comes
into contact with a possible food source, it sends out its
pseudopods, its false feet, surrounds the food, and takes
it into its food vacuole. The amoeba then either absorbs
the food—after which it becomes indistinguishable from
the amoeba itself—or rejects it.

Women experience some men as having
"pseudopodic egos." Their egos reach out, pull women
into their sphere, incorporate them, and from that time
on the women are indistinguishable from them. (This is
a special occupational hazard of wives and secretaries.)
Once a man "absorbs" a woman, he literally does not
perceive that she is a separate being.

This is different from the many women who extend
their egos by living through their husbands and
children. When pressed, these women always know that
they are separate from their husbands and children,

even when they would prefer this not to be the case. But persons with pseudopodic egos genuinely believe that there is no difference between themselves and others. Women who become involved with men of this type frequently describe their experience as one of having been "devoured" or "swallowed up."

Prime examples of pseudopodic egos are often seen during divorce cases. When the time comes to divide up the property, the woman usually knows what she had when she and her husband were married, what he had, and what they acquired jointly. The man, on the other hand, just assumes that everything belongs to him. He literally cannot distinguish between his wife's things and his. It is the old adage corrupted: "What's mine is mine, and what's yours is mine too!"

No wonder so many women feel as if they are nothing more than men's possessions! And no wonder men become so upset when their wives—or secretaries—try to claim their own possessions *and* their own beings.

Women also see men as unresponsive to their ideas—and this is an accurate observation. Men are very attached to their own ideas. They also appear to be very attached to one another's ideas. Women have long complained that they have difficulty getting their ideas across in professional and staff meetings. We are often left with two choices: we can either propose our ideas ourselves and run the risk of their being rejected, because they came from a woman, or we can give them to men and let them present them as their own. Then, at least, our ideas have *some* chance of being accepted and implemented!

Men will fight tenaciously for their ideas. In fact, men defend their ideas like a lioness defends her cubs. On observing this, I realized that men's ideas really *are* their offspring. Perhaps, then, it is easier for a woman to part with her ideas because she has the capacity to

produce human offspring, while a man's major
production *is* his ideas.

The more we model ourselves after men, the more
possessive we are becoming of our ideas. We are no
longer as willing to turn them over to men. We are
demonstrating more willingness to fight for them and to
claim what I call "conceptual paternity." (I use the
phrase advisedly.) Perhaps, as we pass through the stage
of having to "make it" in the White Male System, we
will move further to a place where we can give birth to
our ideas, nurture them and help them grow, and then
turn them over to others for development and finally let
them go.

## THE PERFECT MARRIAGE: AN AMERICAN FAIRY TALE

Women in this culture are led to believe that there is
only one goal worth achieving in life: the Perfect
Marriage. In this setup, two half-people relate to each
other in a symbiotic fashion. Neither can survive
without the other; neither is his or her own person.
This is what we have been taught to believe is True
Love and is the source of the clichés we use to describe
our spouses: "my other half," "my better half." The
Perfect Marriage wears two faces: the public Perfect
Marriage and the private Perfect Marriage. They exist
side by side and are interdependent. Although the
public Perfect Marriage has been hotly attacked by the
women's movement, the private Perfect Marriage
deserves just as much attention.

In the public Perfect Marriage, the man is the
parent, and the woman is the child. The man takes care
of the woman. He is the one who deals with the outside
world, makes the money, decides how the money will be
spent, and makes all of the decisions (either subtly or
openly.) He gets the car repaired and handles all home

maintenance problems. He takes care of the "little woman."

The woman does not know how to support herself, nor does she have the skills to function in the world. Often, she does not even know how to drive (especially if she and her husband live in a city), and she does not have the slightest idea of how to take care of the car. Finances are a complete mystery to her, and she may not even know what her family's financial situation is. When questioned, a woman in a public Perfect Marriage may say, "He *gives* me money to run the house, and that's all I have anything to do with." Or: "I don't want to be bothered with or responsible for financial matters." Or: "Every woman wants to be taken care of—and I'm no different!" The message she receives from him is that she is weak and cannot cope with the world by herself, but she can be dependent on him, and he will do it for her. He is indispensable. The marriage takes care of his "fragile male ego" by making him look strong and sufficient in contrast to his wife's weakness and dependency. This type of marriage becomes a drain on both partners over the years, especially the man, but many young adults enter into it believing it is the course of true love.

The woman's movement has harshly criticized the public Perfect Marriage because it forces the woman to become a childlike cripple. There is no chance for mutual support or mutual respect to grow and flourish in a marriage like this. The woman never has an opportunity to discover herself and her own capabilities, and the man can never take the time to relax and enjoy his humanness. Both partners suffer.

The private side of the Perfect Marriage has received less publicity over the years, but it is definitely present and equally as important as the public side of the Perfect Marriage.

The Private Perfect Marriage goes on behind closed

doors. As soon as the man enters the home, the roles reverse. He may be in charge on the outside—publicly—but home is the woman's domain, and in it she rules supreme!

In the privacy of the Perfect Marriage, the woman is the parent and the man is the child. She feeds him, clothes him, and picks up after him. Often, he does not even know how to choose his own clothes—and may not even know what styles he likes or what sizes he wears. It is the woman's "job" to take care of all of his bodily needs. She makes sure that he looks good. She makes sure that he eats well. She takes care of his sexual wants. She protects him from the children and their noise—he is *much* too busy and important to be bothered! She is responsible for maintaining communication and intimacy in the relationship. She is indispensable.

The Perfect Marriage results in two half-persons who could not survive without each other. Publicly, it appears that the man is a whole person and the woman is a dependent, childlike cripple. Privately, though, it is the other way around. Both partners have to keep up two separate sets of appearances—one for the world, and one for the home.

What happens to Perfect Marriages? Some go on forever in a cling-clung fashion, but others do not survive. It can be that one of the partners begins to grow up. Any number of things may initiate the growing-up process. The husband may take a sensitivity training seminar at work. He may begin to realize that he can become a whole person with feelings, too. Or he may meet a woman who is a whole person and experience what it means to have a relationship with an adult (instead of a parent or a child).

The wife may begin to read literature from the woman's movement or join a consciousness-raising group. She may decide to go back to school or get a job outside the home. She may decide that she wants to control her own money. She may meet a man who relates to her as an equal rather than trying to parent her or be her child.

In either case, one of these two parent-child people starts growing up, and the Perfect Marriage cannot tolerate the stress. It must dissolve or it must change.

Another circumstance that can cause the breakup of a Perfect Marriage is the one in which one of the partners forgets where she or he is and confuses the role she or he is supposed to play. This circumstance is slightly more complicated and confusing. Perhaps the woman behaves like a parent in a situation in which she is supposed to behave like a child. Or perhaps the husband acts like a child during a time when he's expected to take the parent role. (A Perfect Marriage is very rigid and static and must remain that way in order to survive.) This forgetfulness and role-switching can be amusing from the outside, but it feels deadly serious to those involved.

I once counseled with a couple who had decided to go into therapy because she had simply forgotten what she was supposed to do and when. She always cut up his meat at home because she wanted to make sure that he did not have to trouble himself too much while he was eating. One night they went out to dinner with his boss. She forgot where she was and absentmindedly reached over and started cutting up his steak! This embarrassing incident precipitated a crisis in their Perfect Marriage, and eventually they sought counseling.

While outwardly stable, the Perfect Marriage is inwardly so tenuous that almost any incident can take on crisis proportions. Maybe the husband comes home and tells his wife that she should try a new detergent that the "girls at the office" have recommended. This may seem minor, but it is not. How can he tell her what to do at home? The home is her domain. She makes decisions here. He has no right to try to take control here too.

An implied contract has been broken. He agreed to let her take care of him and the house—even though it is supposed to appear as if *he's* taking care of her and the house. They both agreed to go along with the charade. As we have seen, adherence to the charade is necessary for the survival of this rigid agreement.

Whole persons cannot tolerate Perfect Marriages for long. They prefer marriages in which tasks are shared and who does what is determined more by individual competence and preference than by rigid role definition. Whole persons require relationships in which they are allowed to grow and take risks while nurturing and supporting their partners. The Perfect Marriage, the American Fairy Tale, is a refuge for half-persons.

## THE QUESTION OF WHO GOES FIRST

One aspect of male/female relationships that causes a great deal of difficulty has to do with the question of who is supposed to initiate and who is supposed to respond. Who makes the first move? Who says the first crucial words?

Traditionally, men are expected to be the initiators and women are expected to be the responders. Subtly, of course, women often let it be known that it is time for men to start initiating! Ideally, though, men are supposed to break trail and women are supposed to follow.

The initiator is the one who controls the relationship. Surprisingly, this role is often assumed by the person who is willing to *touch* first. The politics of touching is an important issue that women are just beginning to understand.

Several years ago, a paper on the politics of touching was presented before the American

Psychological Association. The general thesis was that the person who touches another first within a particular situation immediately gains the power and control. (Touching is also used to *maintain* power and control; bosses in general feel much freer to touch their secretaries than secretaries do to touch their bosses.)

A man in the audience stood up and began expressing opposing ideas. Without saying a word, the speaker—a woman—left the stage, walked up to him, and firmly grasped him on both upper arms. The man was appalled!

The next day, a complaint several pages long, was delivered to the suite of the Association of Women in Psychology. In it, the man stated that he felt as if he had been raped in public! The woman speaker had dared to touch him first. If he had touched her first, would he have felt like a rapist? Probably not.

The issue of who should initiate and who should respond is a problem in most male/female relationships. The man carries the onus of initiating even if he does not want to, and the woman bears the burden of waiting for the opportunity to be responsive. She is rarely encouraged to initiate a new direction that might be better for both of them.

This results in all kinds of games. If a woman is skilled in handling men, she must set up situations in which the man moves in a direction she has already determined while simultaneously convincing him that it is his idea. (This, of course, protects the fragile male ego.) Or a man must always take the role of initiator even when he would rather not. Neither partner can be honest or whole.

The controller-controllee question can take over every aspect of a person's life. I once heard a woman say, "Whenever I'm walking with a man, I never set the pace. I'm afraid of insulting him!"

# NESTERS, HELPERS, NEW-AGE MEN, AND OTHERS

Many books and articles have been written suggesting that men are natural gypsies and women are natural nesters. This myth has been closely tied to biological functions, such as childrearing, and sociohistorical functions, such as hunting and food-gathering.

Something is happening to challenge this myth, however. This is seen by the fact that the divorce rate is increasing—and not only because more men are seeking divorces, but because more women are. Fewer newly divorced women are getting remarried right away, while divorced men are quickly finding other women to settle down with.

Surprisingly, *women* are becoming the gypsies while *men* are becoming the nesters! Women are feeling more free to try out new life styles and move around, while men are marrying women who will make nests for them.

I am not trying to quell one stereotype by proposing another. I am not saying that men or women are "naturally" anything at all. Men do like nests, though. And if they can keep talking women into being nesters, they can get their needs and wants provided for. In fact, I wonder if men have not tried to convince us that we are natural nesters so that we will provide them with nests.

Another stereotype undergoing examination is that of the all-knowing male "helper." Many men in the helping professions—psychiatrists, psychologists, and counselors—are having a great deal of difficulty accepting the possibility of a Female System. There are times when only another woman really understands what it means to grow up female in this culture. Men do not want to face the truth that there are indeed some things they do *not* know and do *not* understand. Since their identities are so closely tied to their jobs, and their jobs are supposed to involve helping others, they cannot accept the fact that there are certain areas in which they really can be of no help. The pain of this emerging awareness is difficult to observe. Some men try—they try very hard—but there are occasions when women must turn to other women for help and understanding.

There are also New Age Men. They become very spiritual and concern themselves with higher levels of consciousness. Sometimes they even call themselves feminists.

Many women have met New Age Men and gladly fallen in love with them. They are wonderful! They are just like us! They speak to us in a whole new language and try to convince us that they understand us completely. They look us straight in the eye and talk about feelings and emotions, sensitivity and trust. They cry at movies. Some of them even howl with pain and torment. They maintain that they like strong women, especially those who are sexually "free." They are beautiful—at least they think they are. They may wear beads, beards, or gowns. They almost always have a far-off, mystical, holy look in their eyes, and they see themselves as the prophets of the New Age when men and women will truly be equal.

New Age Men are very sensual. They have discovered that women are much more willing to go to bed with men who talk about feelings. Beware! New Age Men are wolves in sheep's clothing.

Finally, there are growing numbers of men who do not fit into the White Male System. Theirs is a valiant struggle. More and more of them are getting together by themselves to explore themselves and their world and to become aware of how they are affected and controlled by the White Male System. They are discovering that having to be superior, and godlike, and all-knowing and understanding can be too much of a strain. They are seeking alternatives to the White Male System, and some of them are succeeding.

These are the men to watch for. They are the ones to whom women will be able to teach the Female System. Fortunately for us all, their numbers are increasing.

# CHAPTER FOUR
# STOPPERS

## KEEPING WOMEN IN THEIR PLACE

A number of techniques are used to make women back off from their own perceptions. I call them *stoppers*. A stopper is anything that keeps us where the White Male System wants us to be. Whenever we overstep our bounds or become "uppity women," there is nothing like a good stopper to make us grab our solar plexus and run!

Stoppers come in many different forms. Some—like rape, battering, and incest—are blatantly physical. Others are more subtle and play on our most tender and vulnerable emotions.

The greatest stopper of all is the implication that a woman is sick, bad, crazy, stupid, ugly, or incompetent. For example: "You are really off the wall!" "Where on *earth* did you come up with *that* idea?" "You just don't understand, do you?" "You just don't know how things *are.*" "How could you possibly believe (care for, imagine, etc.) *that?*" "You've lost your mind!" As soon as we hear someone saying any of these things to us, we feel as if our cavern has been forcibly torn open. We are terrified of being sick, bad, crazy, or stupid—and most of us, deep down inside, believe that we probably are.

Since we live in a culture where our perceptions are rarely validated—especially not by those who "count"—it is difficult if not impossible to trust ourselves. If our perceptions cannot be validated, then we must be crazy. There must be something wrong with us if we do not accept the common reality of the White Male System. Only since women have started talking to one another—*really* talking—have we begun to realize that we have another reality.

It is very difficult for men to understand how fragile our trust in our perceptions is, how easily we can be talked out of them, and how terrified we are of being labeled sick, bad, crazy, or stupid. We are especially susceptible to outside opinions that we are ugly. An ugly woman has no credibility in our society. No one even wants to look at her, much less listen to what she has to say!

From the perspective of our own Female System, we are beginning to take some of the stoppers that are used against us and reinterpret them. I have long been interested in the "you are out of your mind" stopper. In thinking more about it, I have decided that it really is not as negative as I first believed. To be "out of one's mind" literally means to be out of the rational and logical and into one's being. It can mean being "right" with oneself. It can be a delightful and meaningful place to be in this overintellectualized culture.

Guilt is another major stopper for women. Because we constantly bear with us the Original Sin of Being Born Female—of being inherently "wrong"—we readily accept the *corporate* guilt of the world. Whenever a woman is not fulfilling her prescribed role or doing what is expected of her, she can easily be made to feel guilty. Guilt is an effective method of control and frequently is used to maintain the status quo. After all, to be born "a wrong" is to be born guilty.

Since we are taught that our primary role is that of caring for others, we can be made to feel guilty as soon as we start caring for ourselves. How can we be so selfish? Our ability to care is finite, is it not? If we devote some of it to ourselves, how can we be sure of having enough left over to give our husbands and children?

Whenever women start discussing issues that are important to them, someone in the group will inevitably say, "Think of the poor men! They don't have it so good either!" This stopper immediately evokes guilt feelings and fears of being labeled a man-hater. Interestingly, the assumption is somehow implicit that if a woman is concerned about women she is not concerned about men. When confronted with this charge, we typically reassure one another that we do indeed care about men and have not abandoned our roles as their caretakers just because we care about women, too. We spend so much time defending ourselves that we become distracted from other more important issues.

Another guilt-inducing stopper is "Think of all the other needy groups in the world!" "What about starving children, orphans, poor people who live in ghettos, etc. etc.?" (As if at least half of the people in these groups are not women!) What is implied by statements like these is a hierarchy of suffering. Women have no right to focus on their concerns as long as there are other people who need help—and there are *always* other people who need help!

Sometimes we hear that women's issues are not as important as those of class or race because the women's movement is a white, middle-class movement and "real" oppression is economic oppression. We have our cars and homes and healthy children and refrigerators full of food. What are we complaining about? So what if we are only losing our soul?

Yet another stopper emerges when women become more confident and continue their journey toward self-discovery and definition. At this point we tend to become more joyful beings. We laugh more, enjoy life, and recapture the art of playing. This upsets the White Male System, which responds with comments like "I can't stand all this silliness!" Or, "What are you women so happy about lately?" Too much joy is a threat to the System, which does its best to quell our joy and make us feel guilty about feeling joyful.

Women's understanding can also be used against them. As I mentioned earlier, we put a great deal of effort into understanding every situation in which we find ourselves, especially interpersonal relationships. True understanding, though—at least the way the White Male System defines it—cannot involve feelings or emotions. Once we understand a situation, we must not allow ourselves to be angry, resentful, or upset about it. And if we do, we feel guilty.

This often occurs as we explore our feelings about our mothers. Once our consciousness has been raised about women's issues, we can better understand why our mothers did some of the things they did. We get angry, but our understanding tempers our anger. We are taught that understanding—like love—is always gentle and kind. It is never angry or resentful or jealous.

We encounter the same thing in our relationships with men. When we understand how men are also destroyed by the system, we tell ourselves that we are not supposed to feel angry about their part in our oppression. Our understanding stops our feelings and causes us to give up our perceptions.

There is another stopper I like to call the "Great Humanistic Leveler." This is most frequently and adeptly used by men in the helping professions. As soon as we start opening up to them, they take on an expression of deep concern and sincerity. Then they say something like, "Let's not talk about women's liberation. Let's talk about human liberation instead. There are already too many things that divide us. Let's not look at the ways in which we're different. Let's focus on the ways in which we're alike!" This sounds so reasonable and humanistic that we are immediately tempted to fall for it.

Unfortunately, though, the only persons who can really afford the luxury of these sentiments are white men. They do not need to explore differences because they run the system. When we are deprived of the freedom of exploring what it means to grow up female in a White Male System, we are robbed of our experiences and our souls. Our differences give us our identity.

We whites tried to use this stopper on Blacks during the Black revolution. "Let's not look at our differences," we urged. "Let's look instead at our similarities." Once we are dissuaded from embracing the uniqueness of our differences, we start backing off from our own issues and focusing on common concerns. This restores order to the universe—and restores us to the position of meeting the needs of the White Male System. In our culture at least, universal concerns and White Male System concerns are one and the same.

There is an interesting corollary to the Great Humanistic Leveler that I have heard expressed any number of times. It has to do with the assumption that there is no difference between men and women. When someone treats a woman differently, he (or she) is accused of being discriminatory and robbing her of her equality. This stopper is also used by men in the helping professions, especially if they want to get sexually involved with their clients, and it goes something like this: "I have to believe that this woman is an adult and can take responsibility for her own actions—just like a man. If I don't, then I'm not treating her as an equal." Although he feels that he has the power to assign equality (he has, after all, in the past!), he does not have the power to dictate the internal feeling. Whenever I

meet a man with ideas like these, I remind him that
equality cannot be *externally* assigned until it has been
*internally* perceived.

Another effective way to stop a woman completely
is to call her an aggressive female or a castrating bitch.
Men who stand up for themselves are competent and
assertive; women who do the same are obnoxious and
aggressive. Men who openly express different opinions to
women are forthright and honest; women who do the
same are castrating bitches who have no regard for the
fragile male ego.

The "castrating bitch" label is especially confusing
because it introduces a sexual component that seldom
has anything to do with the situation at hand. What
does asserting ourselves have to do with a man's
genitals? The label *sounds* so terrible that we frequently
back off from our own perceptions because we do not
want to threaten or insult a man's anatomy or virility.
We know how important a man's genitals are. They
ensure his innate superiority; without them he is
worthless, just like the rest of us. Along the same lines,
calling a woman a dyke or a lesbian can also stop her
from exploring and utilizing her own perceptions. We
even draw back from liking other women because we are
afraid of being given this label. More and more of us are
refusing to let it intimidate us, however.

Another stopper that is frequently used against
women goes like this: "You're so *serious* these days!
Whatever happened to your sense of humor?" (We are
not allowed to feel joy, but we must always keep our
sense of humor!) Just because we have stopped laughing
at dirty jokes and other slurs against women does not
mean that we have lost our ability to laugh altogether.
Just because we take our concerns and issues seriously
and genuinely care about them does not mean that we
have lost our sense of humor. Again, the implication is
that we cannot have one without the other. If we are

serious about our issues, we cannot be unserious about anything else.

We will also back off from our perceptions when we are ignored or isolated. Token women in organizations often experience this problem; the men they work with every day simply do not hear what they are saying. These women then feel invisible and wrong and set about trying to "reappear" by blending into the White Male System.

The fear of being abandoned is yet another stopper Whenever a woman begins to express her own ideas or demand her own rights—whether in a business situation or a personal relationship—the man she is with may panic. She sees this as an indicator of his imminent withdrawal from her, and she is frightened into silence and conformity.

The so-called Feminine Mystique is also used against women. We often see men shake their heads as they say, "You are so mysterious that I can never understand you!' The usual implication in this statement is "So why try?" If women simply cannot be understood, why should men try to understand them?

Another offshoot of this attitude is what I like to term the "Cesspool Question." We are doing our best to help men understand us when they throw up their hands and say, "What do you women *really* want anyway?" This is not an answerable question! We try to respond and realize that there is no real interest in the answer. The trick is to get a woman to take one step forward as she tries to answer it. She has stepped right into the cesspool and is covered over with shit.

My answer to the Cesspool Question (after spending years doing my best to explain what we really want and never succeeding) has become, "If you ask the question, you will never understand the answer." The issue is not one of information-getting but of trying to prove that women *do not* know what they want. Any attempt at an answer is futile.

Up until now, I have been describing some of the emotional and psychological stoppers that are used against women. There are physical stoppers as well. One of the simplest—and most effective—is touching. As I mentioned earlier, the person who touches another first frequently ends up controlling the relationship. A gesture apparently as innocent as a pat on the head or an arm around the shoulders determines who is in charge.

One of my woman friends is a well-known feminist who frequently interacts with congressmen. She has observed that one way men gain control over women is by calling them by their first name and putting a heavy, passive hand on their shoulder. So she has started doing the same thing. Often she ends up in situations where she and a man are both standing there with their hands on each other's shoulders with no simple way of extricating themselves. They resemble two bucks with their antlers locked—and the scene is pretty comical!

Sheer brute strength is an obvious physical stopper. Women are rightfully concerned about men using physical means to force them away from their issues because so many do just that. Some men may simply resort to rape or battering, but others are more subtle. A very large man may, for example, walk right up to a woman so she is forced to look up at him—to understand. An administrator at a large university was known to threaten to slug women if they did not shut up! He also liked to pick up petite women and carry them around—totally undercutting their sense of authority.

A different kind of physical stopper—but one that can be equally difficult to resist—is comforting. A hug, feigned sympathy, or an understanding look can distract us from entering a conflict or trying to make a point. How can we argue with our husbands when they are being so nice to us? Patronizing is part of this comforting syndrome—and it has been used to stop women down through the ages.

There are some men whose very natures make them effective stoppers. One in particular is the soft-sell chauvinist. He is *for* women's rights and considers himself a feminist. He bridles when he is labeled a sexist or a bigot. How can he be so misunderstood? Doesn't he say all the right things? Doesn't the fact that he tries so hard mean anything to us heartless women?

We do our best not to hurt his feelings. He is one of the few men who really tries to understand us, so we should never alienate him. If what we are saying or doing seems to upset or threaten him, we stop. He tries so hard. He is like the white liberal who does his best to get to know Blacks and their problems while really expecting them to pay attention to him. However, Blacks are generally more comfortable with their own system than women are with theirs. Blacks just ignore him and go on with what they are doing.

Many stoppers are used to quell our incipient feminism. Oddly enough, though, feminism itself can be a stopper—especially when it is used against women by men or even other women who espouse women's liberation. To be told "You are not a true feminist!" can paralyze a woman who is concerned about her own rights and those of all women. The result is that she backs off from her own perceptions and issues and the movement loses her contributions.

I have seen many of the concepts expressed in this book used against women. "You have bought into the White Male System. You are not a feminist!" When feminist or Female System ideas become dogmas to which all women must conform or be labeled sick, bad, crazy, stupid (or, even worse, counter-revolutionary), then they become stoppers, too.

Anything can be a stopper—a word, a phrase, a hug, a slap. The only thing two stoppers may have in common is the fact that they reopen a woman's cavern and abort her process. Stoppers by definition inhibit growth and change and maintain a closed system at the expense of the women (and men) in it.

Women may also shy away from developing mature and independent identities because they fear the loss of innocence. In the White Male System, women are expected to maintain their innocence and trustfulness while men are expected to know the ways of the world. If we, too, gain access to this knowledge—if we bite the apple—then we will lose our innocence.

Innocence is good. Our culture could use more of it. But there is a difference between innocence *per se* and childlike innocence, or naivete. In order to maintain a childlike innocence, one must never grow up or be aware of one's surroundings. In other words, one can never have one's "consciousness raised." I have seen many women struggling with the feeling that if they begin to acknowledge and recognize the sexism in our culture, they will lose their innocence.

This is often equated with the loss of hope, joy, and romanticism. We fear that if we become "aware" we will no longer be able to hope. We will never be able to "fall in love" again. This is an embodiment of the "either-or" syndrome. Either we must hold on to our childlike innocence, or we will become cynical and hard. Either we must forego growing and changing, or we must accept the fact that we will be alone and joyless forever.

What we forget is that we can have our feet on the ground and our head in the stars at the same time. We can be whole people while enjoying the other wholeness of being in love. None of us wants to give up hope, or joy, or romanticism—and there is no need for us to!

While working with women who are trying to get past this innocence/cynicism impasse, I have discovered that there is a developmental, progressive process that

leads to what I call "innocence with wisdom." We begin
with a childlike innocence (which our culture sees as
appropriate for women) and do our best to be the way
the White Male System wants us to be. We carefully
remain ignorant of politics, economics, racism, sexism,
and so on. We accept the honor—and the burden—of
perpetuating hope, joy, and romanticism. We
systematically avoid coming to terms with the world
around us. We do not want to become hard or bitter!

As we mature into full adulthood, though, many of
us find that the position of childlike innocence is
impossible to maintain. Suddenly, we can no longer
ignore sexist media ads. We can no longer turn away
from exploitation and oppression. We find that we must
begin standing up for the rights of others as well as
those of our children and ourselves. We are plunged
into awareness. And we are terrified!

What happens is that we are faced with having to
make a profound decision. We feel we have reached a
"turning point" of Faustian proportions. Do we ignore
oppression—and in essence perpetuate it? Or do we
grow—and risk losing our childlike innocence forever?
For many women, this choice involves a move into a
state of anger, cynicism, and bitterness. It is important
to remember that this is a *temporary* state and one of
growth. Most women are afraid of being angry, cynical,
and bitter for the rest of their lives once they take the
first step in that direction. However, as we learn to
embrace our anger, cynicism, and bitterness and work
through it, we move into another developmental stage,
the one of "innocence with wisdom." Then and only
then can we be truly hopeful, joyful, and romantic. Not
at the expense of seeing; rather, we can feel free to see
what we see and know what we know. We can trust our
perceptions while remaining open, vulnerable, and
loving.

Women in general have few models of innocence

with wisdom. So we must become our own models. If we are willing to risk, we will surely blossom into joy.

## THE MOTHER/CHILD BOND

Many women refuse to claim their own lives because they are afraid of breaking the bond with their mothers. Before discussing this further, it is necessary to define the levels on which mothers in the White Male System relate to their sons and daughters. These are not *all* the levels that exist in the Mother/Child bond but are some important ones.

Mothers relate to their sons on four basic levels. The first has to do with the issue of innate superiority. A woman's status in this culture is enhanced whenever she bears a child—especially when she bears a male child.

As soon as a woman gives birth to a son, she is responsible for teaching him that he is an innately superior being. A mother takes this responsibility very seriously. She educates her son in the full meaning of his birthright. At some level, she treats him with the deference befitting his station and prepares him to take his rightful place in the world. She had better—because if for some reason he fails, it is all her fault!

The second level has to do with the class issue. A mother may love her son dearly, but he is nevertheless a member of a class that has controlled and oppressed her. As a result, she cannot help but feel rage and hostility toward him.

I think that this is directly related to the difficulty many male therapists experience when dealing with women clients' rage. They feel overpowered by angry women. They describe themselves as getting smaller and smaller while the woman seems to grow to gargantuan proportions and becomes completely overpowering. I believe that this is due in part to the fact that male infants are dependent on large, angry women for their very survival. As soon as they grow up, they do their best to stop women from expressing their anger. The culture has developed many ingenious ways to suppress female anger.

The third level in the mother-son relationship has to do with ambition. Because she is constrained by the White Male System, a woman has a hard time realizing her own ambitions. So she turns to her son and says, "Doors will be opened to you that were never opened to me, and *you had better achieve!*" He is given no opportunity to explore other lifestyles. If he were to become a househusband, for example, he would only embarrass his mother. He must take advantage of the opportunity his innate superiority affords him and *make it!* He does not only do this for himself. He also does it for his mother.

The fourth level has to do with the power to validate. I fondly call it the "I hate your guts!" level. It relates to the fact that no woman in this culture can be a valid human being unless she produces children. Some people believe that this has all changed with the advent of the women's movement, but they are mistaken. Just tell someone that you have decided not to have children, or that you are thinking of having your tubes tied, and see what happens! In order to be considered a valid human being, a woman *must* have children. She has no choice. The power that these little beings—our children—have over us and the fact that they can validate our existence makes us "hate their guts." We love our children, but we hate what they stand for.

Women relate to their daughters on the same four levels—they just have very different ramifications. The first level in the mother-daughter relationship has to do with innate *inferiority* (nor superiority, as in the case of a son). A mother must communicate to her daughter the importance of "knowing her place" in the world. The mother is the cultural instrument for teaching the daughter that she is an innately inferior human being.

There are other people who are glad to help us do this right from the beginning. I have come across a number of these in my own experience.

My firstborn was a beautiful little girl. Every time a nurse brought her in to me, she would say something like, "Well, better luck next time" or "It's too bad that your first is a girl, but at least she's pretty."

When my second child—a boy—was born, the comments I heard were very different. One nurse actually said, "you finally did it! I guess you won't have any more children now that you have your boy."

Neither of my children had done anything to deserve either contempt or praise. They had simply been born—but already they were labeled either innately inferior or innately superior.

Women who do not "know their place" experience much hostility in the outside world. That is why we believe we must teach our daughters how to be "proper little girls." We must carefully instruct them in the ways of "acting like ladies" so they will never incur the wrath of the White Male System. In this way, mothers try to protect their daughters from pain.

The second level is extremely important and has to do with the fact that women recognize one another as members of the same oppressed class. Women establish what I term the "simpatico" connection with their daughters. This bond forms the major source of warmth and strength for the female child. It is our salvation. It saves us and assures us of a connection in an alien culture where we "do not belong."

Women often describe this connection as going from solar plexus to solar plexus and experience it as a life-sustaining force. (I find it interesting that while it has all of the characteristics of the umbilical cord it is attached higher on the body.) This connection is a bond through *suffering*. We tell our daughters, "I know what it is going to be like for you to grow up in this culture. I have experienced it. We are connected through our suffering. Our suffering gives us connection and strength." *In order to be bonded, we must suffer.* If we stop suffering, we are threatened with losing all connection. It's a two-edged sword.

As women reclaim themselves and begin to define themselves from within, they begin to explore the possibility of being fulfilled and happy. This almost always causes strain in the mother-daughter relationship and precipitates panic in both parties. (This is true regardless of who starts to reclaim herself first, the mother or the daughter.) Time and again I have heard women say, "I am beginning to feel better about myself, but I simply have to bring my mother along!" All at once, the mother is deluged with feminist books and materials. She is invited to countless speeches and workshops. Somehow we feel that we cannot go any further unless our mothers are also willing to relinquish their suffering!

We want to keep growing and reclaiming ourselves, but we are afraid that if we give up our suffering we will lose the life-sustaining bond with our mothers. Some mothers, in fact, can only relate to their daughters if their daughters are suffering too!

I had one client whose mother had devoted her entire life to suffering. My client was starting to feel strong and good about herself when she suddenly decided to visit her mother. Her mother simply refused to deal with her in her new self-confident state. The daughter persevered for several days and finally gave up. She became depressed because she and her mother could not connect. At that point, the mother responded to her wholeheartedly. So my client was left with two choices: she could either stay depressed and have a relationship with her mother, or feel good about herself and forfeit the life-sustaining bond.

This dilemma often evokes an intense fear of death. Women feel that if they destroy the bond between themselves and their mothers one (or both) of them will surely die. I have actually heard women making statements like, "If I grow and become happy, I will kill my mother." Or: "If I reclaim my own life, where will my mother get her life force?" We feel such responsibility for our mothers that we believe we must stop our own growth. To give up suffering, if one is a woman, may be tantamount to matricide or suicide. What a terrifying dilemma!

The third level in the mother-daughter relationship—ambition—is also a two-edged sword. On the one hand, mothers give their daughters this message: "Go out and become educated so you can do better in the world than I did!" But—and this is a very important but—they are also saying, "Get married, have children, keep house, and clean toilets—just like I did!" The real message is this: "I do not feel very good about the way I have lived my life and choices I have made. It is your responsibility to validate my life. You must do this by making the same choices I made and do other important things in the world as well."

Needless to say, a daughter can get very confused by all of these conflicting demands. She is expected to be better educated and have a better job than her mother, but she is also expected to be a wife, mother, and housekeeper. This is the only way in which she can alleviate her mother's uneasiness about her own choices. If she refuses, she is seen as repudiating everything her mother has ever done.

The fourth level in the mother-daughter relationship—the "I hate your guts" level—has to do with the fact that even a female child is better than none. A woman must produce some offspring in order to have worth in this culture. Yet she resents the fact that another being has the power to validate her—especially if that being is not only tiny but innately inferior.

Some couples base their entire marriages on the relationships they had with their mothers. Perhaps they both hated their mothers or their mothers hated them. This becomes the bond between them. If they ever reach the point at which they start working through their "mother issues," they often discover that they have no basis for relating and must either go their separate ways or start over again from scratch.

The issues I have discussed above are not the only ones within the mother-child relationship, but they are so rarely discussed or understood that they must be important! Taken together, they serve as one explanation of why women fear their own power, their femaleness, and their capacity to stop suffering and be whole, happy people. If we do become free and independent, we run the risk of being punished or rejected by both men and other women. We may even sacrifice the all-important bond between ourselves and our mothers.

## GIVING RED RAGE THE GREEN LIGHT

In my work with women, I have discovered that many of us possess a common fantasy about our rage. When asked to imagine and visualize our rage and its outcome, we frequently picture a lifeless wasteland. There is no living thing; no people, animals, or plants. There is only a wisp of smoke here and there. Everything has been destroyed!

Although we seldom admit it, women firmly believe that our rage is fully as dangerous as an atomic bomb. We are convinced that if we dare to express it or let it out we will destroy everything around us and be left completely alone.

After all, what happens when a woman gets angry?
Men avoid or abandon her. Other women pull away
because their own unresolved rage is suddenly alerted.
She is left alone.

Women are told from childhood that their rage is
inappropriate. It is not "nice" to get angry or violent. It
is not "ladylike." I have come to realize that it is never
*in*appropriate to get angry about being labeled innately
inferior. In fact, I now believe that it is a sign of good
health! Angry or depressed women are much easier to
work with in therapy than those who are numb.

Although women's anger in itself is never
inappropriate, it is almost *always* inappropriate *to the
situation.* I have developed a metaphor that has proven
useful. At birth (or maybe even before), every female is
given a large garbage compactor. We carefully carry our
compactor around with us at all times. Whenever we are
dismissed, put down, or discounted we throw a little
more garbage into our compactor, but we *never express
our anger.* We carefully tuck it away.

As soon as we get permission—or give ourselves
permission—to start letting some of our anger out, we
*never* express only the rage that is related to the
situation. Instead, we dump our entire garbage
compactor. We end up with a huge pile of accumulated
rage—its size depends on how many years we have spent
in this culture—and are immediately confronted with
how inappropriate it is.

Of course it is inappropriate (at least in light of the
situation)! It is not inappropriate to a lifetime of growing
up female in a White Male System, however. Still, we
withdraw in the face of any accusation of this nature
because we know that it has some validity. What
women need, of course, are settings in which it is safe to
clean out their garbage compactors and get help and
support in sorting through their accumulated rage.

As long as I am talking about appropriateness, I

would like to address the issue of what our culture does with emotions in general. We frequently hear that such-and-such an emotion is not logical, rational, reasonable, or appropriate. What is implied here is that the particular emotion is wrong or bad. "You have no reason to feel the way you do." "Why do you let yourself get so upset?" "You're not being reasonable!"

Who ever said that feelings can or should be logical, rational, reasonable, or appropriate? Feelings cannot be categorized. They just *are*. Their very existence legitimates them—nothing else needs to. If someone experiences a particular feeling or emotion, it is legitimate and that is all there is to it. This does not mean—at least to me—that one should go around expressing his or her feelings every time an opportunity presents itself (as some therapists suggest), but rather that it is important for us to "own" our feelings and let them be. They are there, and they have a right to be there.

Some feminist therapists encourage their clients to take out their rage on whatever seems to be causing it—to direct their anger toward their bosses, their husbands, or the White Male System in general. I encourage my clients to own their rage and let it out, but I cannot with a clear conscience suggest that they take this approach. I feel that it is unwise for two reasons: First, it may only be an excuse for the therapist to act out her own issues; and second, it puts the client in a position of being labeled "inappropriate" and subjected to an excessive amount of rage backlash. Women are very fragile in the face of their own rage. They are frightened by it. Instead of letting it out in situations where it may be used against them, they should have safe places where they can go to express it. This can be a therapist's office or a support group setting. Wherever a woman chooses to go, however, she should be able to vent her rage without fear and emerge

88

a little less burdened by it.

## WOMEN IN THERAPY: PROCESS AND PROGRESS

When I first started getting interested in women's issues, my main concern was that of finding ways of improving women's therapy. I felt that women in general were not involved in good therapy and that much of the so-called help they were getting was directed toward convincing them to adjust to the White Male System and accept their assigned roles within it. There were very few therapists who actually understood women, and most of the theories about female psychology were developed either by men or by women who were trained to think in White Male System ways.

I am still very concerned about women's therapy. Although it has moved in some positive directions in recent years, I am still not convinced that it is focused on helping women to become healed, fully-functioning individuals. I am not saying that the majority of therapists are malicious—just ignorant.

What is good therapy? What should its underlying philosophies be? What can heal, and what can hurt? These are some of the questions I have been exploring. As a result, I have developed an approach which I call "Process Therapy." I will deal with a very few of its central issues here.

In order to work effectively with women clients, a therapist must have a thorough knowledge of the Female System and the White Male System. She—or he—must understand what it means to grow up female in our culture. She—or he—must understand that many of the experiences a woman has during her life stem from the fact that she is a woman and may or may not have anything to do with her personally. They are certainly not related to her incompetence, obnoxious personality, or stupidity. Of course, women do exhibit traditional psychological problems but it is very important for the therapist to be able to differentiate between cultural issues and psychological issues.

Therapy for women must also confirm the "female experience," whatever that may be. In the past, "reality testing" has often meant testing out the White Male System reality, which may have nothing at all to do with the Female System reality. The therapeutic process must validate the woman's experience of her own reality and help her to know and understand it.

Women should never be talked out of their perceptions. If a woman feels that she is discriminated against at work, then of course she is! If she feels that she is married to a male chauvinist, then of course she is! She lives in this culture, does she not? As her perceptions are validated, she will begin to trust herself. She will become more willing to clarify and check out her perceptions with less fear of recrimination. She will learn to discriminate between those which are valid and those which are not.

A therapist who is working with women must be careful not to have too many preconceived notions or goals. We know so little! If we can only trust and facilitate women's processes, whatever they may be, then we can help women to move through and beyond them.

Whenever I feel ahead of time that I know where a client *should* go and what she *should* do to get there, I am doing poor therapy. I must constantly remind myself to remain open to the woman's own processes. Admittedly, this is very difficult and painful for me at times—especially when one of my clients hates herself. Nevertheless, I have found that when I can truly facilitate her discovery of where she is, she can then move somewhere else.

I am convinced that the therapeutic *process* is more important than its *content*. If the content of a particular set of sessions is that a woman hates herself, and the therapist facilitates her process of realizing it, then the client is much more apt to move away from her self-destructive feelings. What happens is that the process becomes one of supporting and validating the woman instead of letting her know that she is wrong once again.

I have known feminist therapists who cannot bear it when women hate themselves. They try to convince their clients that they are valuable, worthwhile persons in spite of what they are feeling. In these cases, the client again hears an authority person—the therapist—saying, "I know more about you than you know about yourself." And this is very destructive to women in turmoil.

I have not had any clients who have continued to hate themselves after I have encouraged them to go ahead and do so. When this process was validated, they move on. If we can only learn how to facilitate the *process* of therapy, we will be able to help our clients heal faster. Unfortunately, we are far too frequently seduced by content.

What I like to call "body work" (working with breathing and tension in the body) is also necessary in women's therapy. Either the therapist should have some awareness and skills along these lines or she (or he) should work conjointly with someone who does. We must learn how to facilitate the removal of "body blocks"—tenseness, numbness, deadness—in order to get our clients to experience their feelings and work with them constructively. I have found that working with the body's breathing and tension can actually shorten the length of time necessary for therapy.

Finally—and perhaps most importantly—the therapeutic setting must be *safe*. This is the therapist's responsibility. Often a therapist should choose to sit back and listen rather than confront a woman client. Women get enough confrontation outside of therapy.

Therapy will not be healing if all it does is to reinforce
our culture, if it is an authority figure telling the client
(either directly or subtly) what is wrong with her and
what she should be like. In a safe atmosphere, women
can feel free to grow and change at their own pace.
After all, they are paying for the experience! They do
not need to pay to fall in step with the therapist's pace.
They can do that anywhere outside the therapy setting.

Women know a great deal about healing
themselves. They need to be encouraged—not judged.
They need to be set free—not led along. Most of all,
they need to feel good about what they are doing. They
so rarely have this experience that therapists should do
their best to facilitate it!

I have also found that while each woman's process
differs, nearly every woman goes through a number of
similar stages once she begins working on her own
issues.

Women decide to come to therapy for a variety of
reasons. Some are having trouble in their marriages;
some are severely depressed; some just want to find out
more about themselves. During the inital stages, women
often spend most of their time and energy struggling
with their feelings of what it means to be female and
innately inferior. Other issues that emerge include those
of not liking and trusting other women and not valuing
femaleness. These usually go hand-in-hand with feelings
of self-hatred.

As a therapist, I try to facilitate whatever feelings
the client is having and give her the experience of being
accepted as she is. I never tell her what I think she
should be! If women come in hating other women, I
facilitate this. If they come in insisting that femaleness is
inferior, I facilitate this. Of course, I also explore with
them their reasons for feeling as they do.

I often find that women need to have their
perceptions validated very early in the therapeutic

process. Most women have been trained not to trust their perceptions, and they rarely have the opportunity to explore them without being criticized or dismissed. Unless their perceptions are validated, they can never understand other people or themselves because they will continue to back off from the way they see the world.

There is some validity to any perception, and I always make this clear. I cannot emphasize how important this is! Once a woman realizes that her perceptions are not sick, bad, crazy, and so on, her self-esteem increases and she becomes more willing and able to critique her own perceptions.

Women who come in to therapy are often severely damaged. They also have an amazing potential for guilt. This is where women's groups can be very useful. Women are so uncertain of their own perceptions that it helps enormously to have persons other than the therapist to validate them. The group setting affords many women their first opportunity to be in a situation in which they do not have to explain and re-explain themselves.

As women begin to explore their perceptions, they begin to blame. I consider blaming an important part of therapy. We blame our husbands. We blame our families. We blame our parents. We blame the church. We blame the schools. We blame the culture. I do my best to facilitate my clients' process of blaming. I know of no woman who has not had to deal with a sexist husband, family, parent, church, school, or culture! This may not be the entire extent of her problem, or the complete picture, but it is certainly a big part of it. There are elements of truth in all the blaming.

Some therapists either do not allow blaming or cut it off early. They fear that if a client is allowed to "feel sorry for herself" she will go on doing so forever. I have found that just the opposite is true. Whenever I facilitate and support a client's blaming, she gets tired of it much more quickly than I do. I have yet to meet a woman who can go on blaming forever!

Another aspect of effective therapy has to do with the victim position. Some therapists believe that it is not good to let a woman focus on her victim status. I disagree. There is no woman alive who is not a victim now or has not been one at some time. Women are oppressed because they are women and because their perceptions are seen as worthless. Only when they can confront this awareness and all of its accompanying feelings can they stop being victimized.

Once a woman is helped to see that her perceptions are valid and that it is all right to want to blame and feel like a victim, she can begin moving into the rage stage. This is a very important phase in women's therapy, and I have met very few therapists who can work with it effectively without inhibiting it in some way. Most therapists need special training before they can begin to facilitate their clients' rage. Otherwise, it can be a frightening and debilitating experience for all concerned.

If a woman has not been in a women's group before this point in her therapy, she should be encouraged to join one now. There are two main reasons why I feel the group setting is necessary: First, a group can help to mobilize rage feelings and get them out into the open where they can be worked with. Second, and most obvious, a group provides a support system.

Women are terrified of being abandoned by men and other women. They are convinced that this will happen if they start expressing their rage. Part of the group's function is to provide reassurance that this will not happen. Everyone in the group should be committed to staying in it even when the women involved expose the full intensity of their rage. This is absolutely essential!

Within the group setting, each woman should feel

free to go "all the way" with her rage. This will sometimes mean that others will have to provide the psychological and physical controls which will allow her to do so. If she is forced to maintain control at all times, she will not be able to go completely into the depth of her rage.

In some instances, I have found that group restraining can be helpful. I am not talking about the old encounter group technique of "holding" in order to "break out," but of gentle yet firm restraint. This provides women with the boundaries they sometimes need before they can plunge into their anger.

Rage experiences can be terrifying for both the client and the therapist. When they are adequately facilitated, though, they result in such observable changes and growth that one comes to trust and believe in them. Again, facilitation is the key. If a woman is gently guided toward exploring her rage, she will pass through it rather quickly. If the therapist does not know how to handle the situation, it may go on and on.

A word of caution is appropriate here. When a woman is working through her rage phase, her therapist should *never* try to get her to see "the other side." Some therapists feel that it is important to inject concern for others at this point (usually because they themselves are having difficulty dealing with their client's rage and want her to be concerned about them), but this often does nothing but stop the process. The therapist must trust the process and realize that the woman can grow only by first going through it.

Some women have trouble exploring their rage and letting it out because they have never gone completely into it. They may have tapped into it here and there at different times during their lives, but either the effects were so disastrous or the awareness of how much was still left was so intense that they backed off. A woman's first experience of encountering the depth of her rage lets her know that it is not something she cannot handle, that she can move into it and out of it whenever she needs to in the future.

During the rage phase, women will often make statements like, "It isn't fair!" or "I've been duped!" These too should be facilitated. Often, a woman will express a free-floating rage at the world in general. She may feel as if she needs to direct it toward someone or something in particular, but this is not the case. Her experience and expression of it are what count. I once had a client who spent an entire session raging at the Depression because of what it did to her mother.

As a woman confronts her rage stage—especially if she is able to do so within the supportive atmosphere of a women's group—she moves into the next phase of the therapy process. She begins to explore and get to know herself and other women. She begins to define herself from within. She tests out her perceptions and starts listening to and valuing input from other women. She focuses in on her cavern, decides to work on it, and loses some of her fear of it. She begins to like and trust other women and seek their company. She begins to know what it means to love femaleness and other women.

There are some women who become female chauvinists during this stage. A number of therapists (mostly male) have expressed the concern that women might become lesbians at this point. If some do, it is only because they have found the freedom to discover who they really are. In any case, a woman's love for another woman does not at all have to be sexual. Many people seem to be very worried about this. They are missing the point! Women need—and get—the majority of their support from other women during this stage. They welcome the opportunity to communicate and exchange ideas within the Female System. And that is as it should be.

Following this stage, women move into what I call an awareness of the White Male System as a whole. By now, a woman has enough self-esteem to begin exploring ways in which she buys into the system and ways in which she devalues herself. She trusts other women enough at this time to be able to use their feedback and insights, and she is strong enough not to become defensive (at least, not all of the time) when her own White Male System games are exposed. If she is confronted with being too White Male System, she is able to choose whether that system is congruent with her needs at this point or deserves closer examination.

This stage—the final stage in Process Therapy—is where many traditional therapies start! Some therapists feel that it gives a woman power to tell her that she is in charge of her own life. This does not work, however, unless she has passed through the other earlier stages discussed here. When a therapist begins here with a client, the therapy becomes just another experience of the culture. If the client feels victimized and powerless and her therapist tells her that she has power, this is yet another example of how her own perceptions are discounted! She finds herself in one more situation in which she must conform to authority and please someone else whether or not she wants to.

When a woman is free and able to explore the whole White Male System and her part in it, she gradually becomes aware that the System is destructive to men and women alike.

She can then focus on humanistic issues and be concerned about men as well as women. She can begin to articulate her own system. To try to force a woman into humanism before she has reached this stage is nothing short of inhuman.

# CHAPTER FIVE

# THE FEMALE SYSTEM AND THE WHITE MALE SYSTEM: NEW WAYS OF LOOKING AT OUR CULTURE

## DEFINING TERMS: THE VALUE OF "WOMEN'S TALK"

My observations about the Female System and the White Male System come from women who have begun to trust their own perceptions and feel safe in expressing them. I have found that an amazing number of women with very different backgrounds and experiences tend to agree on many of these issues; this points to the existence of a clarity and commonality that are rarely observed or credited.

Far too frequently, women say only what is expected of them or acceptable in this culture. Their input generally falls into one of two categories: "women's talk" and "peacekeeping talk." Women's talk is stereotyped as useless. It is "all anyone can expect from a woman." It is allowed to exist because it does not threaten the White Male System. Peacekeeping talk does not threaten the White Male System either. In fact, it supports its concepts and ideas. It is women's way of demonstrating their understanding of the System and their reluctance to challenge its myths.

Women who have never stepped outside the

pollution of the White Male System almost always
communicate in one of these two modes. Even women
who have begun to trust their own perceptions often fall
back into one of these ways of speaking when they do
not feel safe.

There is another kind of "women's talk," however.
It is the kind that emerges during individual therapy,
groups, and private conversations—situations in which
women feel safe to explore their own evolving System. I
have often been privileged to hear this meaningful and
moving "women's talk." The ideas presented here were
developed with the help of women who were free to
voice their own perceptions. They provide us with a
solid beginning as we seek to define the White Male
Systsem and our own Female System and explore other
realities.

## DEFINING TIME

Whenever I am comparing the White Male System with
the Female System, I like to begin with a discussion of
time.

In the White Male System, time is perceived as the
numbers on the clock. In other words, men believe that
the numbers on the clock are real and that time itself is
nothing more than what those numbers measure. Five
minutes equal five minutes; one hour equals one hour;
one week equals one week; and so on. Time is what the
clock or calendar measures. One who accepts this
believes that it is possible to be early, late, or on time,
and that these concepts have real meaning.

In the Female System—as well as in the other racial
systems mentioned earlier—time is perceived as a process,
a series of passages, or a series of interlocking cycles
which may or may not have anything to do with the
numbers on the clock. Frequently, the clock is irrelevant
and may even be seen as interfering with the process of

time. Early, late, and on time are concepts that have no real meaning.

There is an interesting correlation here between how much one buys into the White Male System and how he or she views and uses time. White women have bought into the System the most, and they are usually within fifteen minutes or so of being "on time" for an appointment. Blacks have bought in second most, and they are usually within a half hour or so of being "on time." Chicanos and Asian Americans tend to arrive within the hour. Native Americans—who have bought into the System the least—may be days or even weeks "late."

This has been one of the most difficult things for the Bureau of Indian Affairs to learn and understand. Traditionally, the white men who run it will set a meeting, and the Native American representatives may show up days later. The BIA people will angrily say something like, "What's the matter with you? You're not on time! You're late!" And the Native Americans will respond with, "What do you mean?" "We are here, and we will stay until we complete the process." That is "on time" for them!

The BIA implies that the Native Americans are sick, bad, crazy, or stupid because they are "late." They do not conform to the White Male System—the "way the world is." If they do not see time as the White Male System sees it, there must be something *wrong* with them. Neither of these approaches to time is necessarily *right*, by the way. Both can be useful. But when one is the way the world is and the other is sick, bad, crazy, or stupid, no one is free to use whichever approach is best for the situation at hand.

Let me illustrate this further with some examples from my own experience. When my son was little, I used to try to have dinner on the table by six o'clock. That meant that I usually started preparing it around

five o'clock, when I got home from work.
Unfortunately, this was just about the time when my
son's internal time mechanism started running down.
He would begin fussing and pulling at me. When I
continued to go by "clock time" and focused my
attention on preparing the meal, I frequently discovered
that I had developed a "growth" on my leg. My son had
wrapped himself around it, hanging on for dear life
while I dragged him around the kitchen with me! One
day I decided to treat time as a process. When I stopped
what I was doing and responded to him, which only
took a few minutes, he toddled off happily and kept
himself amused until dinner was ready.

Neither approach to time was "right." It just
happened that the process approach worked better for
all concerned in this situation.

Several years ago I was an administrator in a
mental health facility, where one of my assigned tasks
was to run the weekly staff meetings. I soon discovered
that the people who got to the meetings "on time" were
not really there at all. Their bodies were there, but their
beings were somewhere else. Those who came late, on
the other hand, were more "present" than the others.

When I investigated further, I discovered that those
who arrived "on time" had frequently stopped in the
middle of something they were doing in order to arrive
at the meeting on the dot. Those who "came late,"
however, were often late because they had taken the
time to complete a task or bring it to a comfortable
resting point before coming to the meeting. When they
arrived at the meeting, they were ready and able to face
the business at hand.

I began a quiet experiment with the group. At the
beginning of each meeting, I asked the staff to sit quietly
and focus on any anxieties or tensions they were feeling.
I then asked them to relate each anxiety or tension to
an unfinished task or process and write down

what they needed to do in order to finish it. If someone felt especially tense or anxious, I would suggest that he or she take some action toward completing the interrupted task. For example, I frequently discovered that my major tension was related to the awareness that I had forgotten to take something out of the freezer for dinner. A quick telephone call home completed the process and freed me to focus on the meeting.

As we continued to do this exercise at the beginning of staff meetings, we began to use our time more efficiently. While it used to take twenty minutes for the staff to get their bodies and beings together, it now took from seven to ten minutes (a significant reduction—and a very worthwhile one, considering that most meetings were scheduled to last only an hour). We took the option of using a combination of process time and clock time, and it worked for us. Had I not suggested that option, I would have continued trying to drag the entire staff into the agenda when they were not ready for it.

Neither approach to time was necessarily "right," but the fact that we were flexible enough to explore new choices helped us to use our time better.

I once read an article in *Time* magazine about the atomic clock at the National Bureau of Standards. (I have long been fascinated by the National Bureau of Standards and believe that it is one of the citadels of the White Male System. At one point, I used to fantasize that real people did not work there. Instead, there was an elaborate hierarchy of inchworms who measured *everything!* When I finally visited it, I discovered to my amazement that it looks like any other building and that real people do in fact work there!) It seems that the atomic clock is the most accurate time-measuring instrument in the world. It sits up on a hill dividing the passage of time into equal segments. Unfortunately, it still has to be reset annually. In spite of its incredible and meticulous accuracy, the atomic clock does not know about the universe. The universe is on process time. (The universe does not know about the atomic clock either!) It is slowing down. So the atomic clock has to be set back a few seconds every year!

Which is better—process time, or clock time? Neither. Both are valid and useful. It is unfortunate, though, when our culture is denied information about process time because the White Male System insists that its way is the way the world is.

Women often find themselves in situations where process time is more efficient than clock time (for example, in childrearing and in relationships). As a result, we have learned to move back and forth between them with relative ease. Unfortunately, the White Male System often makes us feel guilty when we are "late" and implies that we are sick, bad, crazy, or stupid because we do not use time in the "right" way. It is difficult for us to communicate what we know about using time when we are constantly being made to feel insecure about ourselves and our own perceptions.

## DEFINING RELATIONSHIPS

*BEING PEER*
In the White Male System, relationships are conceived of as being either one-up or one-down. In other words, when two people come together or encounter each other, the White Male System assumption is that one of them must be superior and the other must be inferior. There are no other possibilities for interaction.

In working with men, especially business executives, I have found that many men do not necessarily want to be one-up. They just do not want to be one-down. But since those are the only two options in their System, they do their best to go one-up and put others one-down.

In the Female System, relationships are philosophically conceived of as peer until proven otherwise. (This, of course, is only true for women who feel clear and strong and have come to know and trust their own system.) In other words, each new encounter holds the promise of equality. One does not have to be one-up or one-down, superior or inferior; one can be peer.

A major difference between the two systems lies in these basic assumptions about what kinds of relationships are possible. If you can only conceptualize relationships as one-up, one-down, then you will behave in certain ways. If you can conceptualize relationships as either peer *or* one-up, one-down, you will approach them differently.

A few years ago I was living in St. Louis near Washington University and seeing a student in therapy. She was from another midwestern city where her father owned a business. When she informed him that she was seeing me, he decided to call and "check me out." He wanted to find out about my background, my credentials, my philosophy, my fees, and so on. I thought that his need to do so was both appropriate and legitimate. I was a stranger to him, I lived in a distant city, I was counseling his daughter, and he was paying the bill. If I had been in his place, I would have done the same thing.

When he called, I assumed that we would approach each other as peers. He, on the other hand, immediately approached me in a one-up manner. His tone and attitude were one of a superior addressing an inferior. Since I assumed peerness, I did not go one-down but instead offered him the opportunity to interact with me on the basis of equality. There was a slight pause, after which ensued what I call the "relationships shuffle."

When two persons are physically present in the same place, this shuffle is very obvious. For example, let's say that a man and a woman meet and begin a discussion. The man assumes that the woman will go one-down—and when she does not, he does not know quite what to do next. He shifts from one foot to the other and actually moves his body from side to side (sort of like a gamecock). It is almost possible to see in his face what he is thinking: "Oh, my goodness, she's not going one-down! She's supposed to go one-down! What do I do now? *Someone* has to go one-down!" (Pause. Gulp.) "I guess it will have to be me!" At this point, his posture visibly changes. He seems to sink and get smaller, assuming a stooping position and hating every minute of it. He also hates the person who has "made" him go one-down, and this colors their conversation from that point on.

Of course, no one "made" him go one-down. He *chose* to go one-down because that is the way he believes encounters and relationships have to be. If the woman will not go one-down, then he must—but he resents it!

This is more or less what happened during the conversation with my client's father. When I chose to stay peer and did not go one-down, he went one-down.

I happened to be talking to him on a wall telephone. My husband came into the room and started laughing. "What on earth are you doing in that funny position?" he asked. I was leaning over to the side in what must have looked like a very uncomfortable and contorted posture. In response to his question, I whispered very seriously, "Trying to stay peer with this fellow!"

When I had refused to go one-down, my client's father had shuffled and gone one-down himself. I had stooped to "stay level" with him, and he had shuffled and gone one-down again. His belief in his System prevented him from taking the opportunity to be peer with me. All he knew was that relationships had to be one-up, one-down. That was his reality; that was the way he saw the world. He could not relax into accepting a peer interaction, and trying to stay peer with him nearly gave me a backache!

The relationship shuffle is a common experience for White Male System persons. Whenever one of them meets a Black or a woman (a person who is *supposed* to go one-down) who does not go one-down, his only option is to go one-down himself—and he really resents it. Women managers often complain of this. When they do not go one-down, as expected, then the men they are dealing with go one-down, resent being there, and label the women "uppity." This entire process can take place while a woman is just standing there, giving a man the chance to have a peer relationship with her. The man's belief in the White Male System is so unshakeable that he cannot accept what she is offering him.

I think that it is very important to realize how strongly white men believe in their own System and its myths. They are thoroughly convinced that the White Male System is the only reality, that it is innately superior, and that it knows and understands everything. They are also sure that it is totally logical, rational, and objective. As a result, they are severely limited in their ability to take in new information and have new experiences.

I have a woman friend who is a well-known writer and psychotherapist. She once told me that she strongly resents the amount of time and energy she spends in trying to "stay level" with men who go one-down with her. She finds herself constantly either bending down physically or trying to "pull them up" to her level. She is now in her seventies, and it is getting more and more difficult for her to keep changing her posture in an effort to maintain equality with the men she encounters. Recently she said to me, "They will just have to think of some other way to handle this. I am too old for this stooping business!"

*CENTER OF FOCUS*

There is another major difference in the way White
Male System and Female System persons perceive
relationships. In the White Male System, the center of
the universe is the self and the work. Everything else
must go through, relate to, and be *defined by* the self
and the work. Other things in life may be important
(relationships, spirituality, hobbies, and so forth), but
they are never of equal importance; they always occupy
positions on the periphery of the man's life, on the
outside circle.

I have heard women in workshops say, "The one
thing my husband and I have in common is that we
both love him!"

In the Female System, however, the center of the
universe is relationships. Everything else must go
through, relate to, and be *defined by* relationships. This
may be why women have historically not achieved as
much as men. We tend to subordinate ourselves and our
work to our relationships.

I used to think that men moved into the Female
System during courtship. At that time, a man seems to
set aside his self and his work and put the relationship
at the center of his universe. He is unable to think of
anything or anyone but the woman he is courting. He
talks about her at work and may even miss work in
order to spend time with her. He seems totally engrossed
in the relationship. As a result, the woman gets very
excited and starts believing that she has finally "found
one"—a man who understands the Female System! She
happily tells all her friends, "This one is different! He
really is!" She is certain that at last she has met a man
who knows how to make their relationship the focus of
his life, and she is ecstatic.

As soon as the relationship is "nailed down,"
however—as soon as the man is sure of the woman's
affections, and they are either married or have settled

into some other committed arrangement—he goes back to his self and his work. She looks around at how her world has suddenly shifted and says, "I've been duped!" He begins to notice that something has gone wrong and asks, "What's the matter?" and she says, "You don't love me anymore!" He is shocked. "What do you mean I don't love you anymore?" he says. "Of course I do." (You have 180 degrees of my outside circle! What more do you want?) She responds, "Our relationship isn't the center of the universe for you anymore. And that's what love is!" And he says, "I don't know what you mean."

He really *doesn't* know what she means. She knows his System and her own System, but he does not even realize that she has a System.

Some men I have worked with have discussed this with me at length. And they really do not understand it. What I hear them saying is this: "We men don't move into the Female System during courtship. We don't even know what the Female System is. The relationship is a task (work) to be accomplished, and when it is solidified and we are sure of it we go back to our self and our work and business as usual." No wonder the women feel duped!

I once worked with a couple who came into therapy because they (mostly she) were concerned that there was no love in their relationship. Both believed that there had been earlier. When we examined the relationship more closely, it became clear that following their courtship he had gone back to his focus on his self and his work. He had added the relationship to his outside circle where it did in fact occupy a large part of the energy he did not already devote to his self and his work. The relationship was significant to him, but only as it went through, was related to, and defined by his self and his work. It was not significant in its own right.

The woman felt unloved because the relationship did not seem to be central to their lives together. He assumed that the relationship would "heal" once she understood and accepted his System and its *(the)* reality. Any healing to be done, however, depended on their willingness to know and value each system and then make choices as to which was appropriate at what time.

When I was first working on developing these ideas, I presented some of this material to a group of women seminary students. They in turn became furious with me. They did not like what I was saying at all! "For centuries," they said, "women have focused on primary relationships with men in order to establish identity and gain validation. We have given all of our energy to maintaining these relationships and none to taking care of our own intellectual and creative needs. We want this to stop! We want to start paying attention to our selves and our work—and we don't want to be told that we are 'selling out' to the White Male System!"

I stopped to look at this criticism. It is true that women have frequently subjugated or repressed their own creativity and ambition in the service of relationships with men. It is true that these relationships have held positions of utmost importance, since they were established to absolve women of their Original Sin of Being Born Female. And it is true that this is changing.

Over time, I have learned that women move through a number of developmental stages. We first develop primary relationships with men (or actively seek them) in order to gain our identity and absolution from the Original Sin of Being Born Female. These relationships become the center of our universe. Everything else is relegated to the outside circle. We devote our lives to maintaining our relationships with men, and our work, selves, creativity, and intellectual pursuits are all seen as secondary to these relationships and defined by them.

Then, as we become more aware of ourselves and begin to grow, we move into the White Male System.

We put our selves and our work at the center of our universe. We become "selfish"—something women have a great deal of difficulty hearing—and start to put our own needs first. We devote a great deal of time, energy, and money to the process of self-discovery and the realization of our creativity. We become "workaholics." We spend more and more hours on the job. Money, power, and influence become very important to us. We want to "make it," and our criteria for "making it" are those of the White Male System.

During this phase, relationships become less important to us. Some of our relationships may survive in spite of the fact that we spend so little time maintaining them, but others may fall apart. We are beginning to discover our own capabilities, and we say things like, "I am going to make my impact on the world." "I want to make a contribution that people will remember." "I have no time for relationships. I must focus on my self and my work." Some of us become more job-centered than men!

Once we have "made it," however, we sit back and say, "So what?" We look around and wonder, "Is this all there is? It looked so good from the outside, but now that I've 'made it' I'm bored!" We then begin to move back into the Female System—but because we have changed, our concept of the Female System has also changed. It is no longer defined in terms of our relationships with men. It is no longer used *in reaction* to the White Male System. It has taken on an identity all its own.

It seems as if we must first be successful in the White Male System before we can fully and with clarity move into the Female System. During the early stages of our development when we participate in a reactive female system, in which we are not clear about ourselves and our world, we are dependent on men for our identity and absolution from the Original Sin of Being

Born Female. After we move into the White Male System and become successful, we can then return to the Female System from a new perspective.

In the Female System we "come home" to, relationships are still the center of the universe. But these may or may not include primary relationships with men. They *never* include primary relationships with men that give us our identity and absolve us of our Original Sin of Being Born Female. They may include *equal* relationships with men and will almost certainly include close friendships with other women and genuine friendships with men.

This Female System includes a *relationship with the self*—something that was never present in our earlier concept of the female system. Self-awareness and focusing on the needs of the self are not the same as selfishness. We are still aware of and concerned for others. The essence of self-awareness is a tenderness toward and respect for the self which in turn allows one to be more tender and respectful toward others.

Many women never have a relationship with their selves because they have been taught that to do so is selfish. Or they never become aware of any self except as it is other-defined. Some women do acknowledge the presence of an emergent, embryonic self, but they seldom deem it worthy of a relationship.

As women become clearer and develop a sense of self, they are enthralled and amused by it and want to explore it further. Since we do not have much experience defining ourselves from within, others frequently see this process as taking something valuable away from them. This is not the case, however. We are not subtracting anything from those around us; we are simply drawing toward ourselves. By developing a relationship with our selves, we become more capable of meaningful relationships with others. This is a very different definition of "self-centeredness" than that which is experienced by the White Male System. When we make room for ourselves, we can make more room for others!

The Female System we reenter also involves a *relationship with one's work*. Work becomes more than something one does to earn money; it becomes a "life work." It is what we need to do with our life. It means making a contribution which complements the other aspects of our life. It is not profit- and power-oriented; instead, it takes its meaning from creativity, bonding, humaneness, and service.

A woman who reaches this stage of growth—who moves out of the reactive female system, into the White Male System, and then back into the Female System again—also develops a *relationship with the universe*. She begins to have an understanding of how it all fits together and a feeling that life has true meaning. She sees herself and others in relation to the whole. She may say things like, "When I am lying on my deathbed, I think I will look back on the relationships I have had and the connections I have made. These will be the things I consider most important. It will not matter whether I have built a bridge, or written a book, or had a university named after me. I will cherish the lives I have touched and those persons whose lives have touched mine."

The essence of life in the Female System a woman comes home to is relationships—not relationships that define and validate, but relationships with the self, one's work, others, and the universe that nurture and grow. Not static relationships that are neatly categorized and packaged, but relationships that evolve and change, contract and expand. A process of relationships.

Women seem to need a two-step process to reach this stage; they move into the White Male System, and then they move back into the Female System. Men, on the other hand, have only to take one step in order to reach this level of awareness. Since they have the birthright of innate superiority, they do not have to begin by absolving themselves of any original sin or obtaining their identity through someone else. Yet they still have great difficulty taking this single step.

I believe that this is due to the fact that the position of being innately superior and having the self and the work at the center of the universe is very seductive. If one defines everything through the self and assumes that this is the way the world is, it is hard to imagine a world that is *not* self-defined. Men simply cannot conceive of any other way to be. Women, though, seem to get bored with that position after achieving success at it and seek something else. There are, however, some men who want to and do move beyond the beliefs of the White Male System.

I am not saying that either system is "right." I am merely describing a progression that many women seem to follow. It is hard for men to see and appreciate it, however, when it is labeled sick, bad, crazy, and stupid.

## SEXUALITY

Another major difference between the way White Male System and Female System persons view relationships has to do with the issue of sexuality. The White Male System sexualizes the universe. Individuals, buildings, tools are all defined and identified by their sexuality. The most important aspect of a person, whether that person is male or female, is how he or she expresses sexuality. A person is *defined* as heterosexual, homosexual, asexual, bisexual, celibate, etc. Relationships are *defined* as heterosexual, homosexual, bisexual, celibate, platonic, etc. It is assumed that sexuality is present in *every* relationship.

In the Female System, sexuality is not a major identifying characteristic. An awareness of sexuality may or may not enter into a relationship or a situation. If it does, it is usually during the later stages, and it is never all-important.

Individuals and relationships are not the only things that are defined in sexual terms by the White Male System. Buildings are seen as either phallic or female. I was once driving outside Boulder, Colorado, with a friend when we passed a church where another friend of mine was the minister. The person I was driving with—a man—exclaimed, "There's the three-tit church!" I had always thought of it as the Chinese hat church! Neither perception was "right;" they were just very different.

Tools are also given sexual labels by the White Male System. They are categorized as "male" or "female," depending on whether they are penetrating or receptive. In fact, the whole universe is seen in sexual terms. I was walking through the woods with a friend one fine spring day when he suddenly threw up his hands and said, "Ah, sex!" I started and asked, "Where, where?" "All around you!" he said. "The flowers, the butterflies, the grass. Everything is sex!" Somehow the scene looked different to me!

In the Female System, sex is seen as important, fun, and sacred. It is not used to *define* the world, individuals, or relationships, however. When sex is used to define the world, individuals, and relationships—as in the White Male System—the result is a preoccupation and phobic overemphasis on sex for its own sake. For most women, sex is only one aspect of lovemaking. For many men, sex *is* love—and love is sex.

The prohibitions of the church regarding sex and premarital sex are good examples of this phobic overemphasis. Sex is made into *the* most important aspect of a relationship—the one thing that must "wait" until after the marriage ceremony has been performed. This puts all of the other aspects of the relationship—some of which may be far more

important—completely out of focus. Many people end
up getting married solely because they think this will
guarantee them regular and legitimized sex. They soon
find out that marriage means more than that!

I have long been curious about why the White
Male System is so preoccupied with sex and sexuality.
Frequently I make observations about "what is" and
then set about trying to find out the "why." My answers
usually come from very unexpected sources, as was true
in this instance.

I was asked to serve on a panel with a priest and a
minister. The topic of discussion was an exploration of
sexuality and sexual freedom, or the lack of it, in our
culture. The priest had prepared a lengthy "pro-sex"
paper. His basic thesis was that transcendence is an
essential state for the human organism and that orgasm
is the one time when individuals consistently transcend
themselves. Thus, he implied, sex is not only important
but necessary.

Suddenly I understood the meaning of some of my
observations. (I started getting the answers to some of
the "whys.") If one has the self and the work as the
center of his (or her) universe, then one is in a constant
state of self-absorption. But if one has relationships as
the center of her (or his) universe, then one is
constantly focusing on others and, hence, is in a state of
transcending the self. Sex may be a vehicle for
transcendence; it is not *the* vehicle. Focusing on
relationships can be a vehicle of transcendence. That is
why it is not necessary for Female System persons to
sexualize the universe in order to achieve transcendence.

The important thing to remember in all of this is
that both systems have some internal consistency
regarding sex and sexuality. Neither perspective is
"right." Unfortunately, women are more frequently
damaged in the area of sexuality than in any other area.
Because of the importance that men put on sexuality,

the communication between the sexes in this area is confused and disturbing. Few women have a clear understanding of their own sexuality. We are seldom given the opportunity to learn much about it. Instead, we are called upon to support the myths and perceptions of the White Male System and meet its needs. We are told that our own beliefs and perceptions are not valid, and we are exploited and dominated. When sex and transcendence are used to serve the self, this obviates the need for love and affiliation.

## INTIMACY

Any discussion of sex and sexuality must evolve into a discussion of intimacy. In the White Male System, intimacy is approached physically. Men assume that in order to be really intimate with someone they must be physically close. In the Female System, intimacy is approached verbally. Women assume that real closeness involves sharing and discussing their lives.

I once saw a couple in therapy who exemplified these differences. Each had a different intimacy fantasy about their reconnection after an absence from each other. He traveled a geat deal in relation to his work. As he approached home, his fantasy went like this: He would come home from the airport, walk through the front door, embrace his wife, take her directly into the bedroom, and they would make love. Then they would be connected and intimate with each other. Her fantasy went like this: He would walk through the door after his business trip, she would tell him everything she had been doing and thinking during his absence, and he would respond by telling her everything he had been doing and thinking while they were apart. She would share new insights and awarenesses and *so would he*. She would then be ready to make physical love. They might, or might not, but that decision would be made together. The important thing, to her, was that their intimate

connection with each other had been established
through mutual sharing.

He experienced her words as a barrier to intimacy.
She experienced his physical advances as a barrier to
intimacy. When they came into therapy, they informed
me that they had decided to seek help because of *her*
sexual problem! Her husband had accused her of being
frigid—and she had started to believe him!

Neither approach to intimacy is "right." But when
one is the way the world is and the other is sick, bad,
crazy, or stupid, there is little opportunity for two equal
people to come together and explore the richness of
varied approaches. Only when both persons are willing
to recognize and understand each other's systems can
they truly begin to relate and connect. If they are
unwilling—or unable—to do this, both suffer.

## LOVE

Love is also perceived differently by White Male and
Female System persons. In the White Male System, love
is seen and expressed as a series of rituals. In the Female
System, love is experienced as a flow of energy from
solar plexus to solar plexus.

I frequently work with couples who are tense and
confused about the concept of love. The woman often
insists that she feels unloved. The man then counters
with a recitation of all of the things he does for her. He
brings home the money and supports her and the
family. He buys her presents. He takes care of the
children in the evenings so she can attend a class.
Surely she must see that this is what love is all about!

The woman then timidly responds that she still
does not "feel" love from him. At this point, he accuses
her of being unrealistic and a hopeless romantic and the
topic is closed. What more can he do for her? Isn't he
doing his best to demonstrate his love for her? Of
course! He is being the perfect White Male System lover.

While exploring this issue with women, I have found that their perceptions of love tend to be rather vague and tentative. During the first stages of a relationship, women will often complain about not getting flowers, not getting gifts, and not being taken out. They will equate this lack of attention with a lack of love. Their complaints are not really accurate however; they are not at the root of what these women are experiencing.

Women have been convinced that rituals like these are the true expressions of love. Rituals have no meaning, though, unless another element is present as well. That element has something to do with a flow of energy.

When I ask women to come up with a symbol which they think is representative of love, many draw the sign for infinity ( ∞ ). That is because they perceive love as a back-and-forth, cyclical, continuous flow. It moves from the solar plexus of one person to the solar plexus of the other person and back again. During this process, some of the "love energy" from the first person is left behind in the second person, and some of the "love energy" from the second person is added to the flow and returned to the first person.

In addition—and this is very important—this "love energy" is never a finite quantity. In "real" love between two people, new "love energy" is constantly being added to the flow. One always contributes more than one takes. The "old" is still there, but it has been increased by the addition of the "new." Rituals can emerge from this energy exchange and supplement it, but they can never supplant it.

Several blocks can spring up to inhibit this process. A person can send out love energy and find that the person she is directing it to will not let it in. Or the other person can let it in and refuse to take some of it out because of feelings of unworthiness, anger, and so on. Or the other person can take some of it out but not add anything to it. Or the other person can add something to it and then not let it out again. Or the initial sender can block at any of these places when the love energy returns. If the process is blocked in any of these instances, love is not experienced.

Pieces of this process can happen, but it is necessary for continuous back-and-forth flowing, holding, and building to occur for women to experience complete loving. Needless to say, rituals are much more efficient and far less time-consuming!

Both persons must feel somewhat good about themselves in order for this flow to take place. Both persons must be allowed to express love from the modality of their own System. For example, if the man can only perform rituals for his wife and not allow time for the energy exchange, neither of them will experience love. If the woman insists on the energy flow while refusing to acknowledge or participate in loving rituals, neither of them will experience love. The relationship never achieves its full richness, and both persons never achieve their full happiness. Both feel misunderstood and unloved.

A man may indeed feel an energy exchange—but within him and the confines of his own System. His love energy in this case exists solely to serve the self at the center of his universe. He may feel as if he's a very loving person while at the same time neglecting the woman he loves and her System. She then will not experience his energy as love. This is admittedly a complicated process to explain; I am impressed by how many women describe it in similar terms with such clarity.

## FRIENDSHIP
White Male System and Female System persons also differ with respect to how they view friendship. In the White Male System, a friend is someone who can be

relied upon to support the "team effort." A friend is a "buddy," a "pal." In the Female System, friendship involves basic respect, trust, and knowing and being known.

In the Female System, the focus of friendship is verbal intimacy and mutual sharing of one's being. True friends are those who totally expose themselves to each other, sure in the knowledge that to do so is *safe*.

Women are often hurt in relationships with men because they totally expose their beings and do not receive respect and exposure in return. In the Female System, knowing and being known are of utmost importance to friendship. The process of developing this intimacy generates a great deal of energy and excitement. Each person wants very much to know the other. There is a balance present at all times, a sense of equality and purpose.

An acquaintance of mine kept telling me that she and her husband were still friends even though their marriage was in turmoil. I finally told her that it did not appear that way to me. He did not respect her; that was evident from his willingness psychologically to smother her and overwhelm her with his needs. He also had no desire to know her. According to the Female System definition, that was no friendship.

My acquaintance thought about this for a while before realizing that she had been conforming to his concept of friendship—the White Male System concept. As long as she upheld her part of the family's team effort, she and her husband could be friends *on his terms*. When she did not play her expected role, they could not be friends on any terms, especially not hers.

She often tried to sit down with him and tell him about herself, her thoughts, feelings, and insights. He would dutifully listen, but he would not seek out this sharing or participate in it himself. He expected her to give him the friendship he needed, but he would not return to her the friendship she needed.

He did, however, share more of himself with her than with anyone else. Many of the men I see in therapy tell me that they have no one with whom they really share themselves or no one they really know very well except for their wives. The wives, on the other hand, almost always have at least one close woman friend. This friend fulfills their intimacy needs in ways their husbands do not.

Men's friends are usually "teammates" with whom they work or play sports. They may not ever really know them or be close to them. They may not need to be, especially if they see their selves and their work as the center of their universe. I am not saying that this is "wrong" or that the Female System way of going about friendship is "right." I do know, however, that it is very difficult for men and women—especially spouses—to be real friends, and this is a shame.

## PARENTING

Parenting is another type of relationship that is viewed differently by White Male System and Female System persons. In the White Male System, parenting is primarily focused on teaching the child the rules so she or he can live comfortably in the System and contribute to it. The mother is usually delegated to do the teaching, but she is expected to restrict her training efforts to White Male System values and goals. As a result, the child is overprotected and constrained from exploring other alternatives.

In the Female System, parenting means facilitating a child's development and unfolding. The emphasis is not on *making* a child into something, but on *participating* in the child's gradual discovery of who she or he is. Parent and child are seen as working together in this process. It is assumed that the child will have to learn to live in the world and therefore develop some coping skills. If the child is overprotected, then she or he will never learn the skills necessary for survival.

The Female System emphasizes the *process* of growing and becoming. The White Male System emphasizes the *content* of being a White Male System person.

Once, when my son was very young, I saw him running down the street as fast as his little legs could carry him. He rushed through the double doors of our house and carefully closed both of them before he began to howl. He had cut his finger badly on a neighbor's swing, and I could see that it would need stitches.

After we had returned from the doctor and he had calmed down, I asked him why he had not been howling *before* he had come inside the house and closed the doors. He then told me that one of his favorite neighbors, who often gave him cookies, had said that "big boys don't cry."

I was appalled at the fact that my child was already being conditioned to be a White Male System person. I sat down with him and gently assured him that Daddy cried, Grandpa cried, and so on. I wanted him to know that pain and tears are legitimate to the process of being human, that outside definitions of "maleness" are not always those that should control who we are and become. I knew that this was not the last time I would have such a discussion with him. It's hard to be a Female System parent in a White Male System!

COMMITMENT

To conclude this discussion on relationships, I would like to dwell for a moment on the issue of commitment. In the White Male System, commitment means incarceration. In the Female System, commitment means a covenant relationship.

I have often heard men describe permanent relationships in terms of the loss of freedom. Once they have "settled down," they feel that they no longer have the freedom to move or the freedom to make choices in their lives. To them, marriage is not a growth situation—it's a jail term! This is clear from the institution of the bachelor party, which celebrates a man's last night of "freedom" before he enters into a "life sentence."

In the Female System, a committed relationship is a covenant sealed by a pledge. There is no implication that one's freedom is "lost"—only strengthened. Marriage is a step toward freedom, not away from it. In order to make this step, one must be an adult who has freed herself or himself from the baggage of the White Male System. One must know oneself thoroughly to enter into a covenant relationship.

It is important to remember that we are discussing systems and how they define themselves and function rather than individuals. No person is completely "pure" in either the White Male System or the Female System. Some men may use some Female System approaches in their relationships and some women may use White Male System approaches in their relationships.

However, the fact that White Male System persons and Female System persons perceive relationships so differently often makes the success of those relationships difficult. Many unhappy marriages result. In order to change this, we must all be willing to realize that the White Male System is only a system and not reality. We must learn to value the Female System for what it has to offer us all.

## DEFINING POWER

In the White Male System, power is conceived of in a zero-sum fashion. In the Female System, power is seen as limitless.

The White Male System assumes that if one has, say, 20 units of power and gives 12 of them away, he (or she) only has 8 units of power left. The more one shares power or gives it up to others, the less one has for himself (or herself.) There is only so much power available, and one had better scramble for it and hoard it.

This concept of power is based on a scarcity model. I once heard a woman say, "I want to be the best-known feminist in town, and the only way for me to do that is to get rid of so-and-so" (another prominent feminist). She had bought into the White Male System model of power. She had become convinced that there was only so much influence to go around in the area of feminism, and in order to wield enough of it she would have to wrest some from the other woman.

In the Female System, power is viewed in much the same way as love. It is limitless, and when it is shared it regenerates and expands. There is no need to hoard it because it only increases when it is given away.

This difference between how men and women view love—and power—is often evident following the birth of a first child. The husband assumes that love is limited and whatever love the child gets from his wife will be taken away from what is available for him. The woman, on the other hand, finds that she has less time and energy for rituals but more capacity for love.

Similarly, as we share our power, it increases. This is also true with ideas. White Male System persons tend to hold on to, hoard, and try to "own" their ideas. Because their ideas are not allowed to move around and breathe, they stagnate. When ideas are freely given and exchanged—as in the Female System—they expand and change constantly, remaining fresh and alive.

Perhaps power, like love, is better conceived of as being infinite. Perhaps it is better used differently. In the White Male System, power is conceived of to exert domination and control over others. In the Female System, power is conceived of as *personal* power which has nothing to do with power or control over another.

Neither application is "right;" both may be appropriate, depending on the situation. Everyone needs to be free to explore alternative ways of defining and using power.

## MONEY

For many people, money is the embodiment of power. The more money one has, the more influence one will be able to exert over others. It is interesting to note, however, how differently White Male System and Female System persons view and value it.

In the White Male System, money is seen as absolute and real. It has an intrinsic value. In the Female System, money is seen as relative and symbolic. It has no meaning or value in and of itself.

One of my friends has a great deal of money. From time to time, he lends some out. On several occasions in the past, he and another friend (who usually has very little money) loaned money to a mutual acquaintance. My friend was always very upset when the borrower paid back the other person first. He would complain to me and I would try to be sympathetic. I could understand his irritation, but it seemed clear to me that the person with less money deserved to be paid back first. I always felt as if the value of money was relative. Why shouldn't the other person be paid back first? Wasn't the money worth more to him because he had less to begin with and needed it more than my friend?

To most women, money has no meaning at all unless there is something in particular they want to buy.

I was once negotiating with a man to purchase some property. I made an offer that I thought was very reasonable in light of my finances and his investment. He, in turn, wrote a letter back to me in which he accused me of being either naive, stupid, mean, or manipulative.

I immediately knew that our problem could be defined as a systems problem. (I have learned that whenever a string of derogative adjectives are leveled at me, it is usually a systems problem.) I was trying to deal with a White Male System person from my Female System perspective. He attributed absolute value to the money that would be involved in our transaction, while I saw the money as relative to other concerns. He thought that I should pay him precisely what he asked—that was the only absolute he could see.

It was helpful to see that we had a systems problem, and not a personal problem. It was clear to me that I would have paid him whatever he asked, if I could gather the funds to do so, because care for the property and internal integrity were my absolutes.

Women are often told that we have no "money sense" and do not know how to "handle" money. I believe that this is because money is relative to us. We do with it what we want to do. We use it to acquire things we want. Other than that, it has no meaning.

This is clearly exemplified in real estate transactions. Men and women have different goals when it comes to investing in property and real estate. In the White Male System, a sensible investment involves getting a good return on one's money and not paying a penny more than the property is worth. In the Female System, the major issues seem to center around whether a piece of property "feels right." Women will buy real estate if they like it and want to live in it or use it themselves. They are not particularly interested in potential appreciation.

A Female System approach to buying property may not be money shrewd, but it is usually living shrewd. Why buy a house if you would not want to live in it yourself? Women are frequently more concerned with the quality and process of an investment than they are with how much money it will or will not make. Internal considerations are much more important than external ones. As a result, women are often viewed as poor investors. They make too many "emotional" decisions. And an "emotional" decision, as you will recall, is not logical, rational, or objective, but sick, bad, crazy, or stupid.

## LEADERSHIP

Leadership is another symbol of power. In the White Male System, leadership means to lead. In the Female System, leadership means to facilitate—to enable others to make their contributions while simultaneously making one's own.

I have often found executive job descriptions both impressive and amusing. Many of them are written in such a way that only God could fill the position! Unfortunately, many aspiring executives are convinced that they can be God if they want to. (Many drop dead from the effort!) In their System, leading means being out front at all times, having all the answers, and presenting a strong, powerful, and all-knowing image.

In the Female System, a leader's job is to find persons who have particular knowledge and skills and then delegate responsibility to them. Leadership often means nudging people from behind rather than leading them from somewhere ahead. It also includes encouraging others to discover and develop their own capabilities. Although the White Male System does not respect the Female System's definition of leadership, it constantly makes use of it for its own purposes.

## RULES

In the White Male System, leadership involves a thorough working knowledge of the rules. Rules exist to control others and limit their freedom. It is assumed that people are self-centered and power-hungry and need to be kept in line. Rules are a result of a regulatory approach to others, so rules are made to support the System. After a while, if that is indeed what they accomplish, they become sacred. They take precedence over the individual, who must learn them in order to fit into the System and support it more effectively.

In the Female System, rules are developed to increase individual freedom rather than to impose limits. They aim at embracing the individual and serving her or his needs, not those of the System. They are intended to facilitate personal growth. As a result, they are in process. If a rule does not make sense, it can be challenged and modified or even thrown out altogether. Rules never take precedence over the individual.

The best place to learn White Male System rules is on a baseball or football or soccer field, where the good of the team overrides the needs of the individual players. Female System persons seldom make good team members in competitive situations because they will challenge the rules if they do not meet the needs of the individuals involved.

White Male System persons frequently try to manage their families according to System rules. The husband wants to run his family like a "tight ship." Frequently skills that are useful in a work situation are inappropriate in a family setting. He makes the rules and expects his wife to carry them out. Often, however, a family will function more smoothly if it is allowed to operate in a Female System way. Everyone but the husband realizes this, and the result is sabotage on many levels. The woman is forced to undermine her husband by saying things to the children like, "Don't tell your father!"

# DEFINING THOUGHT

In the White Male System, thought is perceived as a linear process. One moves from point A to point B to point C and so on in order to reach a conclusion. In the Female System, thinking is seen as multivariant and multidimensional.

Many studies in psychology that focus on the thinking process have shown these differences. But since they have seldom been designed for this purpose, the data about women's thinking have usually been thrown out or judged irrelevant. In those studies which do set out to discover the differences between men's and women's thinking, the data are frequently interpreted as "proving" that the male thinking process is "logical and rational" while the female thinking process is "scattered."

How data is interpreted—and the language used to interpret it and draw conclusions—often reflects the bias of the researcher more than it does the data. It is important to note the value judgments implied by such labels as "scattered." "Scattered" is different from "multidimensional." Many so-called "scientific" findings about what women are like are no more than reflections of a researcher's White Male System bias. One must look closely at who is interpreting data and what biases or prejudices might be present before one can effectively evaluate the conclusions that are drawn.

Linear thinking is efficient. It allows conclusions to be reached and information to be processed fairly quickly. It is not especially creative, however. Multivariant thinking, on the other hand, takes more time and makes use of more data, some of which—like feelings, intuitions, and process awareness—may seem irrelevant on the surface. But decisions reached by linear thinking seldom "hold" or have the full support of the group concerned, while decisions reached by multivariant thinking do tend to "hold" and have the full support of the group. Neither way of thinking is necessarily "right;" both can contribute to data processing and decision-making.

When doing organizational consulting, I frequently hear women voice a common complaint. It seems that whenever they try to contribute to staff and committee meetings they are accused of "getting off the track," "bringing in irrelevant material," or "interfering with the completion of the task." Usually what is happening is that they are using multivariant thinking. A staff functions best when it uses *both* multivariant *and* linear thinking processes. Women can learn both—they have to in order to survive within the White Male System—but men often have a hard time doing so. I have been paid handsomely to go into an organization and teach its top management what they could be learning for free from the women around them!

When one type of thinking is considered logical and rational and the other is dismissed as sick, bad, crazy, stupid, or "scattered," everyone forgoes the opportunity for creativity and growth. When women are told that their thinking is "wrong," they tend to back off from their perceptions, hold their solar plexus, and either keep quiet or do their best to demonstrate what capable linear thinkers they can be. The organization and the people in it are then robbed of valuable insights and input.

## METHOD OF PROCESSING DATA
Men and women not only think differently; they also process data differently. In general, a man takes in information through the sense organs in his head. It is then sent to the brain, where conclusions and decisions are made, and the brain in turn transmits these conclusions and decisions to the rest of the body for action. This type of rational thinking usually occurs in the left brain.

A woman takes in information through her solar

plexus. It is received and processed there before being sent to the right brain, then to the left brain, and then back into the body for action.

White Male System processing appears to be more like rational thinking, while Female System processing is more similar to intuitive thinking. Female System processing is often slower than White Male System processing, and it is very difficult to support it with logical statements. When questioned about their processing, women can often do no more than throw up their hands and say, "I just feel it" or "It feels right." And men will respond, "What do *feelings* have to do with *thinking?*"

In the White Male System, feelings and intuitive thinking are always inferior to logical and rational thinking. Men find it difficult to trust intuitive thinking unless it can be backed up by a logical statement—which if often cannot be. What we fail to realize is that men *and* women are capable of *both* kinds of thinking. Neither is the "right" way; each has its place. Women have been encouraged to develop intuition because this helps them to cope with their responsibility of pleasing men and their need to get validation and approval. Our intuition is often what tells us how to care for men and make ourselves indispensable, thus ensuring our place. Unfortunately, we are not allowed to carry it over into other spheres, so we must also know how to process data logically in order to survive in the White Male System. Men, on the other hand, only need to know one way of thinking—their own.

## LOGIC
Logic is also used differently in the two Systems. In the White Male System, logic is a tool one uses to win. It does not matter if it is used with internal consistency or balance. In the Female System, logic is perceived as a clear, balanced progression in which both grace and

power are possible.

A client once asked me to sit in as a consultant at a school conference about her daughter, who was very unhappy with kindergarten after two years of attending a full-time Montessori school. My client had requested that her daughter be considered for advancement into the first grade. She was understandably nervous about going alone to see the principal, the school psychologist, the social worker, the reading specialist, and her daughter's teacher—all at the same time! Since I had been a school psychologist for several years, she thought that I might be able to help her through the meeting and add a note of objectivity to it.

Each school person presented his or her thoughts and opinions, after which the mother presented hers. Several questions and answers were shared. Finally the school psychologist—a man who was opposed to moving the girl into the first grade—straightened up and said, "Well, *logically*, if we put the child ahead and it is too much for her, and she then dislikes school and doesn't do well, it will be because we put her ahead." I replied, "Following the same logic, if she is bored with school and kept back and later continues to be bored with school and doesn't do well, it will be because we kept her back."

Both statements followed the same internally consistent logic. Unfortunately, when they were examined side-by-side, they did not make any sense! Two people can follow the same sort of logical thinking process and reach opposite conclusions neither of which may have any validity. The school psychologist was using his logic to win, not to explore the problem.

I have found that in arguments between husbands and wives, the husband tends to begin with a logical rationale for his position. The wife then matches his logical process with her own content, taking care to be internally consistent and true to the process he has established. At this point, the man switches logical frameworks, and the woman is confused. When she, too, switches logical frameworks, she is accused of being illogical! Clearly, the issue is not one of internal consistency but of winning.

## DEFINING COMMUNICATION

In the White Male System, the purpose of communication is often to confuse, win, and stay one-up. In the Female System, the purpose of communication is to bridge (a term women often use), understand, and be understood.

A woman returned home from a nine-day seminar I had conducted on the Female System and excitedly began sharing with her husband what she had learned about communication. Everything she had heard and experienced during the seminar supported what she had been believing for years! She declared that from that point on she was going to say what she meant and mean what she said both at work and at home.

Her husband was appalled. She was a college administrator, and he felt as if he had taught her everything she knew. If she *did* start saying what she meant and meaning what she said, she would surely lose her position of power at the university and jeopardize their relationship at home. According to him, honesty only made one vulnerable. And that could not possibly be the purpose of communication.

Men and women frequently mean entirely different things when they speak of communication. That is why it is so difficult for couples to communicate. A man and wife may have quite disparate goals and never reach the point at which they can explain them to each other.

### NEGOTIATION
Since communication is such an important part of

negotiation, it should come as no surprise that White Male System and Female System persons also differ in what they term negotiations. In the Female System, negotiation is a process that allows one to clarify his or her wants, present them clearly, and willingly listen to what other people want before coming to a mutual agreement. The goal is for everyone to realize as many of his or her wants as possible. Negotiation is fun because it stimulates creativity and imagination that can then be used to facilitate solutions that will be good for everyone concerned.

In the White Male System, negotiation is seen as a way of manipulating others. The goal is to insist on more than one really expects or wants, then bluff, and end up with something close to what one wants. The fun is not in the process itself, but in winning.

Men and women frequently assume that they mean the same thing when they use the term negotiation, but they do not. Since the White Male System is seen as the way the world is, women are usually dismissed as poor negotiators.

## DEFINING RESPONSIBILITY

In the White Male System, responsibility involves accountability and blame. The responsible person is the one who is blamed if something goes wrong. In the Female System, responsibility means the ability to respond. A responsible person is one who does something when it needs to be done, and blaming never enters in.

In my role as an organizational consultant, I have found that much of the tension between management and staff (or, in other words, between men and women) centers around issues of responsibility. The White Male System designs elaborate accountability-blame hierarchies in order to establish who will be blamed if something goes wrong. The Female System functions quite well without this structure.

I once did some consulting with a school personnel office. It had a staff of eleven women and one man and functioned smoothly except for one problem: Each year, the man would leave and a new one would come in. The new one would invariably be disturbed at what he termed the office's "lack of organization." Since no accountability-blame system had been established (it had never been necessary), he would look around and say thing like, "You can't run an office this way!" or "We *must* decide who is accountable and who is responsible!" or "This office will be in chaos if we don't set up an accountablity-responsibility system!" The eleven women would ask "Why?" and settle in for yet another siege. At the end of the year, the man—by then totally frustrated—would leave, and the office would continue on its way. It is interesting to note that it took a ratio of eleven women to one man for the office to operate within the Female System concept of responsibility!

I used to run a series of weekend workshops at my mountain home. At one point, I scheduled couples for one weekend and only women for the following weekend. Several of the same women attended both workshops.

During the couples' weekend, there was always one man at every meal who decided that the group had to get organized or the meals would never be prepared and the cleanup never accomplished. He would set about assigning tasks for everyone. After it had been determined who would be responsible and accountable for what, he and the other men could relax.

This never happened during the women's weekends. Whenever it was time for a meal, some women would prepare what they wanted to and others would clean up afterward. Responsibility and accountability were never even mentioned. It was simply assumed that whatever needed to get done would get done.

The responsibility-accountability issue is often a key factor in determining why a particular organization seems to be breaking down. Since the Female System concept of responsibility—the ability to respond—is rarely seen as valid, women frequently sabotage the White Male System hierarchy in subtle, passive ways.

## DECISION MAKING

Decision making goes hand-in-hand with responsibility, and it is yet another area in which White Male System and Female System persons differ. In the White Male System, decision making follows Roberts Rules of Order. It is assumed that one is born knowing Roberts Rules of Order. Most of us do indeed learn them by osmosis, since they are part and parcel of the White Male System which surrounds us.

In the Female System, decision making is a consensual process. It requires one to take personal responsibility for seeing that issues are clarified and that everyone has a chance to contribute.

In majority (or Roberts Rules of Order) decision making, up to 49 percent of the group can be unhappy or dissatisfied. Depending on how unhappy or dissatisfied they are, they may set about trying to sabotage the decision. In consensual decision making, each individual involved is given the time to reach a personal place where she (or he) can at least go along with the decision and to some extent support it. No policy is set over someone's dead body. The individual good is considered just as important as the collective good.

Consensual decision making is also vulnerable to sabotage. One of the ways in which the White Male System chips away at this process is by instructing a group to go ahead and make consensual decisions after giving it little or no training. When the group fails to

come up with workable—or "right"—decisions, it is
assumed that consensual decision making is ineffective.

Each form of decision making has its place. While
the Roberts Rules of Order type is more efficient and
expedient, Female System decision making is more
creative and tends to result in decisions which have a
better chance of being supported by the whole group.

## PROCESS VS. PRODUCT

The White Male System has a product-goal orientation.
The ends almost always justify the means, and it does
not matter how a goal is achieved just so long as it is.
What counts are outcomes. Men are constantly
arranging their lives into a series of goals.

The Female System has a process orientation. A
goal is less important than the process used to reach it.
We have little difficulty in changing goals and seldom
feel guilty for not attaining our original ones (except
when the men in our lives accuse us of "failing").

One often sees evidence of these differences in
couples who go hiking together. The man sets a goal for
the hike—such as getting to the end of a trail or getting
to the top of a hill—and focuses all of his energies on
reaching that goal. Once he does, he considers the hike
over; the return is simply a "loose end" that needs tying
up. The woman, on the other hand, sees the hike as a
*process*. She likes to stop along the way and smell the
flowers, look at a stream, or just sit. There are times
when she meanders and times when she hikes briskly.
Meanwhile, her husband tells her that she is "lazy,"
doesn't know "how" to hike, and in general is a drag to
bring along and cramps his style. He seldom sees the
valued and legitimate differences in their approach; his
is "right" and hers is "wrong." No wonder women end
up hating to go on hikes with their husbands!

## CONSERVATION-EXPLOITATION

Many of the goals set up by White Male System persons involve exploitation and "using up." In contrast, Female System goals require one to conserve and "live with."

The White Male System assumes that people, animals, and the earth as a whole exist to support and be used by it. Individual needs are overshadowed by the urge to generate more money and more things. A well-known hotel in New York City is a good example of this attitude. It has piped-in heat, piped-in air conditioning, piped-in music, and piped-in smells. One can stay there indefinitely and have no relationship whatsoever with the city environment. (You don't even smell N.Y.C.!) Needless to say, it takes a tremendous amount of energy to keep the hotel running. Then again, controlling the environment—or, in other words, being God—is a primary goal of the White Male System.

The ideal house is one in which the temperature is basically the same all year round. The ideal shopping area is climate-controlled. The ideal automobile is air-conditioned and equipped with a stereo system. Who cares if we must exploit the earth in order to make ourselves comfortable? And who cares if we in turn lose our physical capacity to adjust to changes in temperature, humidity, and so on?

The Female System is concerned with conservation and saving the planet. In that respect, it is very similar to the Native American system. One is expected to become attuned to the processes, cycles, and seasons of the earth—to live and move in harmony with them rather than to control them.

In conforming with these objectives and this philosophy, Female System persons often get involved in ecology issues such as saving the whales, redwoods, and wilderness. They are on the forefront of movements which aim at stemming pollution. Each issue in itself may not be of grave importance, but each has profound symbolic meaning.

As I was listening to the news one evening, I heard about a group of researchers in Washington, D.C., who believed that they had developed the technology necessary to control the weather. All they needed were a few billion dollars more for some final experiments and studies. I was struck by the White Male System thinking and assumptions behind their research—that it would be a good thing to be able to control the weather, and that time and money should be used to reach that goal. My immediate response was, "Why would anyone want to do *that?*" And the answer, of course, was this: to be God. What better way to show off Godlike powers than by manipulating the wind and the rain, the sun and the snow! I could not help thinking that in the Female System money and energy would be put into finding ways to live with the universe, not control it.

Neither approach is "right." Humankind must be able to make use of the resources available to us. But we should not have to rape our planet in order to get what we need.

## DEFINING MORALITY

In the White Male System, morality is a public issue. In the Female System, morality is a private issue.

The White Male System sets about legislating its own morality through politics, economics, and education. It wants everyone to conform to its definitions of right and wrong. It wants everyone to support its myths and beliefs.

The White Male System acknowledges that there is such a thing as private morality but has relegated it to women and the church. As a result, private morality does not have as much power or influence in our culture as public morality. Whenever public and private morality come into conflict, public morality wins. The Nixon years proved this. It was all right to lie, cheat, and steal for the "good" of the country or the Presidency.

The church plays the same role in relation to politics, economics, and education as women play in relation to men. It is there, and it deserves to be listened to from time to time, but in the final analysis it simply does not have as much clout. The White Male System gets very angry when women or the church interferes with its public morality. One sees evidence of this whenever the clergy try to get involved in the "real world." Many people were outraged when ministers "interfered" in the civil rights movement, and the clergy were often the first to be attacked on marches and picket lines.

A good friend of mine was a minister in an all-white church in Georgia several years ago when he chose to take a strong pro-civil rights stand. Although the members of the church loved him and his family and felt good about his ministry among them, they would not accept what he was doing. They pleaded with him to focus on his *ministry* and not bring politics, economics, and education into the church. He saw his ministry as involving both private and public morality. Finally, his congregation asked him to leave, and he did.

## DEFINING HEALING AND IMMORTALITY

In the White Male System, healing is something that is "done" by the healer. The healer must be all-knowing and certified as such by the White Male System. If the healer cannot figure out what is wrong with a sick person, or a certain prescription does not "work," then it is assumed that the person is imagining her (or his) illness. The healer is never wrong!

In the Female System, the healer's role is to

facilitate the flow of helpful knowledge and energy that comes from within the person to be healed. The healer must be knowledgeable, but she (or he) is expected to use knowledge to allow healing to occur.

I once worked as a psychologist on the staff of an adolescent treatment unit at a state mental hospital. Whenever I heard the phrase, "This patient is untreatable," it made me uneasy. I finally realized that for me the right statement to make was, "We do not know how to treat this patient." Needless to say, this created quite a furor within the staff!

In the Female System, healing is a process that occurs within a person with facilitation and help from the healer. Any healing that takes place is based on the relationship between the healer and the patient. In addition, the healer must have a good relationship with herself (or himself) in order to release the healing flow within the patient. Healing never depends on the strength or God-like omniscience of the healer, as it does in the White Male System.

One of the major strongholds of the White Male System today is the American Medical Association. Its myths and assumptions are almost identical to those of the White Male System, and the difficulty many doctors have in differentiating between themselves and God is apparent.

Since White Male System persons so firmly believe that it is possible for one to become God, they are understandably concerned with the issue of immortality. Female System persons, on the other hand, realize that immortality is not a genuine possibility and spend little or no time worrying about it.

Nearly every man I have ever seen in therapy spends several sessions dealing with immortality-related anxieties. As one strives to be God, the issue of immortality poses a number of peculiar problems. If one is mortal (as most human beings are), then the process

---

of becoming immortal becomes a ticklish issue. At some level of their consciousness, though, a surprising number of men really *do* believe that it's possible for them to become immortal. They only have to find the way! At this point in time, however, immortality can be approached by only three avenues: one must either have children, especially male heirs to carry on the family name and bloodlines; or one must amass material goods; or one must produce lasting things like "great books."

The need to ensure one's immortality through children is, I believe, one reason why monogamy is so important in Western culture. When a woman has a baby, she knows whose it is. There is never any doubt in her mind that the baby is hers. Unless she can be convinced that monogamy is essential, however—and this is easy enough to accomplish if she can be made to believe that her connection with a man is the only thing that will absolve her of her Original Sin of Being Born Female—then *the man is never sure that she is carrying his child.* Men find this uncertainty absolutely terrifying. It seems ironic that these potential gods have to be dependent on inferior beings to ensure their immortality. That they are is probably one of the major causes of men's hatred and fear of women.

I have yet to meet a woman who concerns herself with the issue of immortality. She may want her children to validate her own choices, but she seldom believes that they will guarantee her eternal life on this earth. She is usually too busy struggling with more mundane issues such as the need to survive and establish a sense of self-worth.

## SYSTEM VS. SYSTEM: A FEW OPENING WORDS

In light of the observations I have made with the help of women who have felt "safe" enough to explain their

System to me, I feel that I can begin to draw some preliminary conclusions.

The White Male System is in general an analytical, defining system. The Female System, on the other hand, is a synthesizing, emerging system.

The White Male System feels the need to analyze, understand, and explain the world. It does so by taking a whole, breaking it down into its component parts, and defining each of these parts in turn. People and things are seen as being however they are defined.

The Female System sees the world as constantly growing and changing. It cannot be defined; it can only be observed as it emerges. Understanding comes from watching, learning from, and facilitating the process of emergence. One does not need to pick something or someone apart. One does not need to control or define.

Why are the White Male System and the Female System so radically different? Because differences in and of themselves are perceived in radically opposing ways by persons in both Systems.

In the White Male System, differences are seen as threats. In the Female System, differences are seen as opportunities for growth.

When differences are labeled dangerous or harmful, it becomes essential to train everyone to think and act in similar ways. Thus, our educational system is oriented toward the "average" child. Any young person who is found to be "above" or "below" average must be made to fit the mold. Anyone who insists on her (or his) right to be different must be done away with, either literally or figuratively.

Because it refuses to see the worth and meaning inherent in differences and perceives them as threats to be overcome, the White Male System is a closed system. It stifles creativity and devours itself from within. It wastes and loses energy and is moving toward a state of entropy.

Because it perceives differences as opportunities for stimulation and growth, the Female System has been nearly eaten up by the White Male System. Women have recognized the White Male System as different from their own and sought to learn from it. But our genuine curiosity and interest—not to mention our need to survive—has backfired. We, the subordinate and inferior people, have embraced the System of the dominant and superior ones—but our own System has been ignored or undermined.

This is not intended to be an exhaustive or all-encompassing discussion of the two Systems. I see it as only a beginning, as one step in a process and progression toward understanding one another and our world.

Often, as I share my concepts and theories with other women, they beam at my descriptions of our System. Many have said to me, "This is the first time I have ever heard someone say aloud what I already know!" Women rarely hear about their System, and when they do it is usually in derogatory terms. It is important for both women *and* men to know and admit that the Female System exists and is good—not necessarily better, but good.

It is also important for women *and* men to see that the White Male System is just that—a system. It is not reality. It is not the way the world is. Reality is difficult if not impossible to change, but a system can be changed, even if it means a struggle. That gives us hope. If we can learn to recognize that there is at least one other system besides the White Male System, we can begin to see the value of still other systems and realities. We can begin to pay closer attention to the Black, Chicano, Asian-American, and Native American systems and learn from them as well. It is only then that we will begin to grow to our fullest capacity as human beings.

# CHAPTER SIX
# PARADOX, DUALISM, AND LEVELS OF TRUTH

## NOTHING IS BUT WHAT IS NOT

Thus far, I have focused primarily on the *content* issues of the Female System and the White Male System. In order to have a fuller grasp of the two systems and how they function, though, one must also examine them in terms of their *processes*.

The first process I want to explore here is paradox. The White Male System has little or no understanding of paradox. Paradox is not linear, and it cannot be measured by numbers. Yet some of the most profound philosophical concepts ever imagined in this world are expressed in paradox. Who has not heard that "one must lose one's life in order to find it?" How many of us really know what this means? Before one can begin to get a solid grasp on paradox, one must be willing to relinquish both intellectual and physical control. That is very difficult for White Male System persons to do.

I have come to believe that paradox is one of the keys to psychotherapeutic healing. The only way to get out of a depression is to go into it. The only way to deal with rage is to embrace it. In the process of owning our rage, we can accept it, value it, and work through it to the other side.

Since most therapies are linear and have been developed by men, few of them make any use of paradox. Paradox cannot be completely understood by the left brain. A great deal of right-brain intuition is necessary. Using paradox is the same as heading east in order to reach points west. The path may be longer, but the process of getting there is sure to be more exciting and stimulating or at least different than the direct route. Using paradox is like trying to think of a name long forgotten. If we think hard about it, we can rarely force the name into our consciousness. But if we go ahead and do other things, the name will suddenly appear like a light behind the eyes. This is neither a rational nor an intellectual process. It simply happens. One must trust the paradox of not thinking about thought if one really wants thought to occur!

All of the major world religions emphasize the importance of surrender. In its own way, surrender is paradox. To seek power is to lose it. To surrender power is to gain it. It may not be the same sort of power we were looking for to begin with; it may be worth even more.

Paradox often emerges in childrearing. If we try to control and hold on to our children, we lose them. If we let them go, they return to us more fully.

It is very hard for White Male System persons to allow paradox to take its place in their lives. Doing so implies a certain lessening of control, and it is difficult for a superior being to go along with this.

Women delight in paradox and find it stimulating and enhancing. When we experience paradox, we do not care who is in control. We tend to be less concerned about control than men anyway (since we have so little to begin with), so we are more open to the paradoxes of daily living. We realize that there is no one truth—and that all truth is one!

As the White Male System opens itself to the process of paradox, it too will become less concerned about power and control and more open to experiencing the enrichment paradox offers.

## THE EITHER-OR SYNDROME

The White Male System is a dualistic system. It thinks in dichotomies and believes that the world must be viewed in that way. We are trained to perceive things dualistically and to simplify the world into "either-ors."

No one would deny that this type of thinking is efficient. In the previous chapter of this book, I presented the content issues of the White Male System and the Female System in a dualistic fashion. That was an efficient format, and I feel that it worked. I *chose* to use this format, however; I did not do so because I assumed that the world is broken down dualistically and everything must be viewed in this way.

Down through the ages, humankind has spent a great deal of time and energy speculating on the existence of a dualistic world. Yin and yang are dualistic concepts, as are right and left, good and evil, up and down, black and white. Sometimes it is very tempting to look at the world as a collection of "either-ors." If something is not this way, it must be that way. Anything in between is irrelevant.

I once presented these ideas to a group of students at an intellectually-oriented, private midwestern college. As I began to challenge dualism, one of the male students became very agitated. "You can't say those things!" he claimed. When I asked him what in particular was upsetting him, he replied, "We *have* to think dualistically. There is no other way to understand the world around us. Besides, if what you are saying is true, then everything I'm learning is wrong!" (A dualism right there!) He was a junior with a major in philosophy and logic, and he was being taught to think and explore the world dualistically. No wonder he was agitated by what I was saying!

Because we are so thoroughly trained in dualistic thinking, we can use only a small fraction of the capacity of our brains. Our brains have the capacity to function like computers. We can process many kinds of information from many directions, but it all comes out looking like the binary system: 1 or 0, off or on, either-or. Just imagine what we could do if we used our full potential! We humans take pride in how far we have come on the evolutionary ladder, but to limit our minds to dualism is to crawl when we can run or even fly.

Dualism is one of the most frequent causes of faulty communication between White Male System and Female System persons. Recall that earlier I defined Female System communication as bridging. Rather than either-or, communication becomes either-*and*-or.

Whenever I lecture on this material and say, "Women are not inferior. They are truly wonderful!", someone in the audience almost always responds, "Why do you think men are inferior and why don't you like men?" In dualistic thinking, affirming one side of a dualism is tantamount to attacking the other. When one person differs with another and says, "I am right," the other automatically assumes that the first is really saying, "You are wrong!" Often, when I find myself in this situation, I will agree to the other person's "rightness" as well as mine. The Female System is not a dualistic system. It allows two people to be right even when they differ.

Once a dualistic assumption is made and the dualistic thinking process is engaged, conflict and misunderstanding usually ensue. One cannot value women and men too. One must choose—and one had better make the "right" choice, leaving the other to be labeled "wrong," since two differing rights are conceptually impossible.

I am not saying that we should throw out the dualistic thinking process; it is simple and efficient in a

number of situations. I am only saying that it does limit
creativity and cause a great deal of unnecessary
confusion. I have found it very helpful to point out
dualistic thinking processes when they occur during
conflicts and to seek other ways of going about finding
solutions. (And I do my best not to say, "We must *either*
think dualistically, *or* . . .!")

In fact, I have discovered two simple methods
which have proved very effective. The first involves
thinking quickly of other alternatives to the two
(dualistic) ones that have already been proposed. When
someone says that we either have to do this (1) or this
(2), I try to add that we could also do this (3) or this (4).
This process seems to break down the dualism rather
quickly. I also find that others can generally come up
with possible solutions (5), (6), and (7) on their own,
further facilitating creativity and growth.

The other method involves nothing more elaborate
than changing the word "but" to "and." Frequently,
people will say, "I agree with you *but* . . .," and this will
engage the dualistic thinking process. I suggest that we
change the statement to, "I agree with you *and* . . . ."
This opens the conversation to negotiation without
pitting two people against each other in a win or lose
(that is, dualistic) situation. I have found that this tactic
can make impressive differences in communication and
reduce unnecessary conflict.

In order to break down dualism, one must of course
be willing and eager to find alternative solutions to
problems and differences. If one insists on winning and
being one-up, he (or she) will tenaciously adhere to the
dualistic thinking process.

As we go beyond the dualism of the White Male
System, we open new doors to understanding. As we
free our minds to think multivariantly, we develop the
ability to find complex solutions to complex problems.
As we begin to understand and see dualistic thinking for

what it is, we can choose between it and other realities.

## TRUE, TRUER, TRUEST

Of all the perceptions and awarenesses that have emerged from my work, I believe that the levels of truth concept is one of the most important.

Many of the problems we have communicating with one another have to do with the fact that people speak from different levels of truth and are often unaware of other levels. I like to diagram the concept in this way:

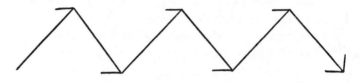

When describing it verbally, I delineate several aspects of it:

1. Every issue has its own levels of truth. Levels of truth move in a progression. As one grows and increases in awareness, her or his levels of truth move from the superficial to the more profound.

3. When a person is operating from a particular level of truth, that level is "true" for her or him.

4. A person must fully embrace the level of truth she or he is on before moving to another level (a paradox!).

5. One can understand and sympathize with various levels of truth *if* she or he has passed through them.

6. One cannot understand or sympathize with those levels of truth through which she or he has not yet passed nor those which are beyond her or his current level.

7. The further along one is on the levels of truth continuum regarding a particular concept, the better

able she or he will be to understand the concept itself and the levels of truth others are at concerning it.

8. As one moves along the levels of truth, each new level is almost always the opposite of the previous one. Although this gives the appearance of inconsistency, it actually represents a growth in awareness.

9. When one looks only at two adjacent levels of truth, they may give the appearance of a dualism, or dialectic, but this is not the case. Nevertheless, they look that way when one views them statically and not as part of a process.

10. Although several levels of truth may look *behaviorally* similar, they are *attitudinally* very different.

11. Unless one is able to understand and appreciate different levels of truth, she or he will not be able to communicate effectively.

Since all of this is initially a lot to absorb, I will illustrate with an example.

Some time ago I was invited to be the keynote speaker at the First National Conference on Human Relations in Education. I was also asked to be the conference evaluator, which meant that I was expected to attend and critique the various workshops offered at the conference.

The first workshop I visited focused on the gay issue in education. The people who were there ranged from those who (supposedly) did not even know anyone who was gay to those who identified themselves as such.

We were asked to participate in a simple exercise. We were each handed this grid and asked to fill in the spaces with terms that applied to each group.

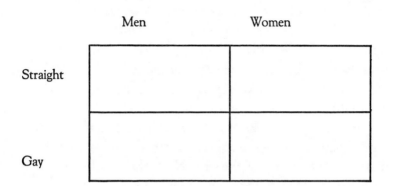

|          | Men | Women |
|----------|-----|-------|
| Straight |     |       |
| Gay      |     |       |

When I looked at the results of this exercise, I found that the people in the workshops were operating at four different levels of truth. In graphic terms, the group looked like this:

Level 1 persons did not even recognize that such a thing as "gayness" existed and had no terms to describe it.

Level 2 persons knew that there were gays in the world but had very little information about them, so they were threatened by the concept of gayness. In some circles, these people would be described as extremely homophobic. Their awareness of gays had congealed into a number of terms which they used in a derogatory and bigoted way: dyke, queer, faggot, queen, lesbian, etc.

Level 3 persons considered themselves "enlightened" and "liberal." They recognized and acknowledged gayness and had worked through at least some of their homophobia. They knew about gay rights and did not want to say anything that might be construed as offensive. So they "cleaned up" the language they used to describe gays and tried to correct their bias against them. Terms like "dyke" and "faggot" had been excised from their vocabulary.

Level 4 persons had worked through much of their homophobia. Some had both gay and straight friends; some were gay themselves; they had moved beyond the ostrich phase (Level 1), beyond the homophobic phase (Level 2), and beyond the liberal phase (Level 3) and were fully aware of all three previous levels. Those who had gay friends felt comfortable fondly calling them "You old dyke" or "You old faggot." The terms had taken on an endearing and affectionate tone and were a natural part of their language.

There are several important and interesting observations to be made here. The first has to do with *directionality*. As people become more aware of gayness, they tend to move from Level 1 through Levels 2, 3, and 4. (There were no Level 5 persons in that particular group. Level 5 would probably include people who did not identify persons by their sexuality, did not use the terms, and so on.)

The second observation has to do with the fact that it is difficult if not impossible to return to lower levels of truth after attaining higher ones. A Level 4 person could never again be a Level 1 person on this issue, and it is doubtful that a Level 3 person could return to Level 2 thinking.

The third observation has to do with the fact that everyone will fight for the "rightness" of her or his own level of truth. The vehemence and intensity of their conviction tends to decrease as they move along the various levels simply because they are able to look back at the ones they have already passed through. The most outspoken and "bigoted" persons in a group are usually those who are still at the earlier and less aware levels of truth on a particular issue.

It seems to me that a person who is at a less aware level of truth is much more insecure about her or his convictions and therefore demands that others agree with her or him. Those who have gone through more levels of truth, however, tend to be more tolerant and open-minded. They can understand the levels they have passed through themselves and envision other levels in the future, even if they do not yet know what they will be. Persons at the highest levels of truth are often lonely because the further one moves along, the more people one leaves behind.

Looking back at the diagram, it can be seen that Level 2 moves in the opposite direction of Level 1, Level 3 moves in the opposite direction of Level 2, Level 4 moves in the opposite direction of Level 3, and so on.

This leads to the fourth observation: each new level of awareness almost always moves in a different direction from the previous level. This means that as one grows in awareness, she or he presents a picture of inconsistency. Something I hotly defended last week may no longer be true for me today. And something I defend today may not be true for me tomorrow.

Since two adjacent levels of truth move in opposite directions, they have the appearance of a dualism when viewed together. It is very limiting to view levels of truth in this way. Instead, one must perceive them as stages in a dynamic process. The movement toward greater awareness is not limited to any two levels of truth; instead, it is comprised of many levels progressing toward more and more wisdom and understanding. It is important to avoid being seduced into a dualistic conflict of right or wrong by those who can see only two levels at any one time.

The fifth observation may be the most fascinating. It has to do with the fact that each level of truth bears a strong behavioral resemblance to the one two behind it or two ahead of it. They are quite different attitudinally, though.

In this example, Levels 1 and 3 look very much alike in behavioral terms. Level 1 persons are unaware of "gayness" and as a result have not developed a language to describe it. Level 3 persons have "cleaned up their act" and do not want to offend or behave like bigots, so they do not use the language they acquired back in Level 2. A person from either of these two groups would never say the words "dyke" or "faggot." Behaviorally, then, they appear to be much the same.

Their attitudes are radically different, however. Level 1 persons know nothing about gays (and would probably prefer to remain ignorant.) They have little or no understanding of the levels of truth on this issue. Level 3 persons, on the other hand, are definitely aware of gays and gayness. They also have a beginning understanding of the levels of truth process.

Levels 2 and 4 also look behaviorally alike. Persons from both levels use identifying terms for gays. Attitudinally, however, they are diametrically opposed. Level 2 persons use the terms disparagingly. Because of their homophobia, they look on gayness with hostility. Level 4 persons have come to terms with at least some of their homophobia and use the terms warmly (as happens when two Blacks fondly call each other "nigger"). Level 2 persons despise gayness; Level 4 persons are comfortable with it and accept it.

Persons from both Levels 2 and 4 are often hotly attacked by those from Level 3. In their attempt to be liberal and affirm their own level of truth, Level 3 persons will attack anyone who uses the terms. They turn on Level 2 persons for being close-minded and bigoted. They attack both Level 2 and Level 4 persons for using the language and do not perceive the attitudinal difference. They only perceive and defend their own level of truth.

As people move along the various levels of truth, they are less likely to attack those who are still at the levels through which they have already passed. When this does happen, which is rare, it is usually related to the fact that one must fully affirm one's own level before she or he can progress to the next.

In my experience, I have found that levels of truth emerge on almost every issue or concept. When people have trouble communicating, it is usually because they are operating on different levels and do not see themselves as participating in an ongoing process.

Needless to say, the levels of truth concept poses a serious challenge to the belief that there is *one real truth* about any issue. If each level of truth is in itself real, then the process of moving toward greater (different) truths must be one of expanding awareness (as in the Female System) rather than that of merely seeking a goal (as in the White Male System).

Paradoxically, one must fully embrace and affirm each level of truth before moving on to the next. If one tries to move too quickly through the levels, she or he gets stuck. And if one refuses to move on to a new level when it is time, she or he stagnates.

The approach to wisdom is a ripening and ongoing process. Wisdom in itself is a process, not a product!

I have found that the levels of truth concept can be applied to all issues, big or small, important or unimportant. Let me illustrate this with another less significant example.

As a pre-teen I was unaware and did not care that many women shaved their legs (Level 1). When I became more sophisticated, I shaved my legs and underarms like most women of my generation (Level 2). When I started getting involved in the women's movement, I let the hair under my arms and on my legs grow (Level 3) as a political statement that women (and I in particular) were just fine the way they were naturally. Then, as I became aware that I did not want a movement to dictate to me any more than I wanted the White Male System to, I started shaving my legs and underarms again (Level 4). Today, I find that I like to let the hair on my legs and under my arms grow during the winter—it makes me feel warmer—and shave it during the summer to feel cooler and sunnier (Level 5).

Although this example hardly carries the weight of the earlier one I gave, the two of them are similar in many ways. As I moved through my levels of truth on the shaving issue, I was open to attack from persons on the other levels. I had more tolerance for the levels I had already been through than the people in them did for me. I am totally unaware of how my next level will evolve (Maybe I will turn into a monkey!). Each level felt "right" when I was in the midst of it, and I trusted myself enough to withstand the criticism I got and fully embrace it.

All too frequently, our culture's prophets, philosophers, and critics forget the levels of truth they have passed through and try to impose the distillation of a more advanced level on the rest of us. At times like these, we must remind ourselves that true wisdom involves helping persons through their own levels *at their own pace.* Theologians and people of the church are often guilty of pushing people toward levels beyond their present capacity. They have forgotten that wisdom is a process and are doing their best to advertise a product. We can only embrace that which we really know. A highly evolved "product" is useless unless it has real meaning for us.

# CHAPTER SEVEN

# AN INTRODUCTION TO FEMALE SYSTEM THEOLOGY

## THE IMPORTANCE OF BECOMING THEOLOGICALLY AWARE

I have no intention of embarking on a complicated and involved theological discussion in these last few pages. I will leave that to the "real" theologians—women like Mary Daly, Carol Oachs, Patricia Kepler, Rosemary Ruether, and others—who are eloquently raising issues that challenge and relate to the White Male System. Instead, I will address issues that have seemed important to me as I have worked toward an understanding of the White Male System and the Female System.

I believe that it is absolutely essential for men and women in our culture to be theologically aware. We cannot ignore theological beliefs and still hope to understand what is happening to men and women today. Women in particular are very strongly affected by the theological assumptions of the White Male System. We must recognize this as we move toward fuller knowledge of our own System; to ignore it is to remain ignorant.

I also believe that any therapist who plans to work with women or couples must become thoroughly versed in the prevalent theological assumptions. Refusing to do this is unfair to their clients.

I recently ran a nine-day workshop for women, several days of which were devoted to discussions of sexual histories, awareness, and identity. I noticed that in almost every person who attended there was a constant interplay between her experiences with her sexuality, her theology, and the church. The three were as inextricably interwoven in the individual women as they are in our culture.

When I first started working with this material with different groups, I used a simple exercise to generate information. I would draw two columns on a chalkboard and head one *God* and the other *Humankind* (otherwise known as Mankind), after which I would ask the people in the group to brainstorm terms describing God and Humankind in relation to God. (I should mention that I used this exercise in corporations and government agencies as well as in churches.)

After listening to various mumblings—"I don't believe in God," "What's the purpose of all this?"—I would reassure the group that no assumptions about belief or the lack thereof were intended. I just wanted to know what they knew about God. Sometimes I got some rather unusual responses. Once when I gave the Mother's Day sermon at a Unitarian Church on this topic, a big burly man stood up and said, "God was the mean old bastard who gave Job all those sores and boils." I quickly nodded and asked if we could abbreviate his response to "mean old bastard" before adding it to the list!

At any rate, I usually got the same clusters of responses regardless of who my audience was. Even those who hotly claimed to be agnostics or atheists could tell me exactly what "He" is like! Most people would begin describing God as I always expected them to: male. They would then move on to the omnis: omnipotent, omniscient, omnipresent. Finally, they would add the other common descriptors: immortal, eternal.

No one ever listed any of the omnis under Humankind, though. Instead, they came up with labels like these: childlike, sinful, weak, stupid or dumb, and mortal.

Following this, I would draw two more columns on the board and head them *Male* and *Female*. I would ask the group to brainstorm more terms, specifying that these should describe males and females in relation to each other. When these lists were completed, they almost always looked something like this:

| Male | Female |
|------|--------|
| Intelligent | Emotional |
| Powerful | Weak |
| Brave | Fearful |
| Good | Sinful |
| Strong | Childlike |

When all four lists had been completed, I set up the columns in this way:

| God | Humankind | Male | Female |
|-----|-----------|------|--------|
| male | childlike | intelligent | emotional |
| omnipotent | sinful | powerful | weak |
| omniscient | weak | brave | fearful |
| omnipresent | stupid or | good | sinful |
| immortal, | dumb | strong | like children |
| eternal | mortal | | |

What evident conclusion can be drawn from all of this? That Male is to Female what God is to Humankind. When humans are compared to God, humans fall into the weak and sinful category. But when men are compared to women, men fall into the godlike category and women fall into the weak and sinful category. (There seemed to be some confusion about what to do with the immortal-mortal issue, though most of the group probably would have added immortality to the Male list.)

This sets up the basic mythology of the White Male System. Our theology supports these myths. Men believe that they can be God, strive to achieve godhood, and die in the process. Women have no chance of ever becoming God and try to relate to these mortal gods—men—in an acceptable way.

It is interesting to note that *every* group I tried this with came up with essentially the same ideas. These assumptions and myths go deep into our culture and give great validity and support to the White Male System—more than one would suspect.

Our culture is set up according to this basic hierarchical structure:

God
Men
Women
Children
Animals
Earth

God is dominant over men, women, children, animals, and the earth. Men are dominant over women, children, animals, and the earth. Women are dominant over children, animals, and the earth. The earth is at the bottom of the hierarchy; it is seen as powerless and submissive.

Along with this dominance goes a tendency to rape and control those who are below one in the hierarchy. There is also a feeling that one should constantly strive to move upward to the next rank; that one's present position is never good enough. Men try to be like God; women try to be like men; children try to be like adults. We also try to force those below us in the hie archy to be more like us.

I have already discussed at length what happens to men who try to be like God. The strain is too much for their bodies, and they die prematurely. Women who want to "make it" in the White Male System strive to be as much like men as possible. For a woman to be told that she thinks "like a man" is perceived as a high compliment. We try to turn our children into adults ahead of schedule by saying things like "Be a big boy!" "Act like a lady!" "Big boys don't cry!"

I once heard on the radio that a fifth-grade boy had been expelled from school. My curiosity was piqued, and I decided to find out what a fifth grader could have done that was so terrible as to incur expulsion. When I talked with the teacher, she claimed that the boy had not been "acting his age." He had been cutting-up in class and being playful instead of settling down. It was clear to me that he had been acting *his* age—he had just not been acting *his teacher's* age. He had been kicked out of school as a result.

Adults are constantly giving children the message—either directly or indirectly—that they are not okay simply because they are not adults. When one is a child and being a child is not acceptable, one forms deep feelings of confusion and low self-esteem. When one is a woman and it is not okay to be a woman, one forms deep feelings of confusion and low self-esteem. None of us can help what we are—yet we are told that we must keep trying!

We also try to make our pets more human. We refuse to appreciate their basic "animalness." Many of us are probably guilty of saying something like this: "Oh, my dog doesn't know he's a dog. He thinks he's human!" And we accompany this ridiculous statement with a foolish smile. When I was in graduate school, I had a friend whose two Siamese cats used the toilet. He derived great prestige from that fact.

This, then, is the setup: Those at the top of the hierarchy dominate, and those lower down must either strive to move up or be dragged up by the scruff of the neck. Yet men cannot be too much like God or they die. Women cannot be too much like men or they are shoved back down again. Children cannot be too much like adults or we no longer find them entertaining. What a mess!

What one *is* is never enough. The very structure of most theological assumptions results in this dominance-submission scheme. Power is at the top. Total powerlessness is at the bottom. It is possible to become more powerful by dominating those below you and standing on their shoulders; this is a common and acceptable practice.

What people often neglect to realize is that this hierarchy results in an assumption of an unchanging God. God must remain constant so men can strive to be like "Him." The hierarchy itself must also remain static. One must focus on goals and content, never on process.

At times, these assumptions seem quite amusing. How could an unchanging God be responsible for creating an ever-changing and expanding universe? Still, there is a belief that there must be an ultimate truth somewhere. Otherwise, the hierarchy crumbles. If instead we move along levels of truth, then what happens to men's position in our culture? What, in fact, happens to our culture?

At this point, one must take another look at the concept of transcendence. Is the key to transcendence paradox? In order to transcend oneself, does one have to fully embrace and be who one is (in other words, human)? If one constantly strives to transcend, does one miss who one really is? As we become more fully human, do we become more transcendent?

These are not easy questions. The reason people keep asking them is because no one has ever come up with satisfactory answers. Then again, the majority of people who have attempted answers have come from the White Male System. Does the Female System have something to teach us here? I think so.

I also think that we need to become clearer about the assumptions and effects of theology on our culture so we can better understand the issues women and men face. The theology we know has been developed to support the myths and assumptions of the White Male System. A number of liberation theologians have already suggested this. Is it possible to filter out the White Male System assumptions? Some women theologians are doing their best. They are exploring the issues of patriarchy and matriarchy and going beyond what they have been taught to think and believe.

A friend of mine, a Native American theologian, once said, "When we concretize our perceptions, we are participating in theological idolatry." To become rigid and static is to become an idolator. To establish and maintain a static hierarchy and a static system is to participate in theological idolatry.

Without a doubt, the church has perpetuated the concept that the suffering servant is the holiest person of all. Women and minorities have been encouraged to be suffering servants, thereby achieving absolution. But when we put ourselves in dependent, childlike, or subservient positions, we deprive others (God and men) of the experience of relating to mature adults. The White Male System is a father figure who requires all others to be dependent on it. God is seen as a father who focuses on control and controlling. One is either controlled or controlling, depending on where one is in the hierarchy.

In the Female System, god is viewed as process. Process is never constant or static. Our natural, human process is god—yet god is *not* just our process (paradox!). To live and follow our personal life process is to be with god.

In the White Male System, living in tune with God means getting in tune with something outside the self. God is static and good. One is expected to reshape oneself according to these external criteria of goodness. In order to be attuned to God, then, one must learn to deny or transcend the self. One must strive to be what one is not.

In the Female System, living in tune with god means being in tune with what one already *is*. God is changing and growing. One must only stay in tune with one's process to remain attuned to god. Our true selves are never in conflict with god. And god is not *just* our process and god *is* our process.

Idolatry is the abortion of the process of being, and sin is alienation from that process. Women are often accused of being selfish when we cease to focus solely on others and begin to respect and follow our own process. I have observed that whenever a woman (or a man, for that matter) is in tune with her own process, she never harms herself or others. She may do things that others do not like or appreciate, but she does not harm them. When we are out of tune with our internal process, though, we distort ourselves and are often destructive to others. That is the true meaning of sin.

The issues of control and controlling have no place in Female System theology. Neither does domination, since persons are expected to facilitate their own processes and those of others. Facilitating, by definition, is never harmful and always helpful.

Female System theology is process. It is hard to nail it down, separate it into its parts, and assign each part a description or definition. What I know about Female System theology is what I have learned from the women I have been privileged to talk with over the years. They have shared with me their own spirituality. They have felt "safe" enough to ignore what they have been taught

and what they think they should believe and delve
instead into what they know and intuit from their own
experience. What has emerged is what I have briefly
discussed here. It may not be logical or rational or
objective. It is, after all, the product of multivariant and
multidimensional process.

As we learn to see our present theology as a
product of the White Male System, our understanding
of theology will deepen and change. As we seek to know
and be known, will we have to accept assumptions or
realities or both? Even though the White Male System
has no theology of differences, will we feel free to
explore that which is different? Will we be able to open
ourselves to learning the Female System, the Black
System, the Native American System, and other systems
as well?

Differences challenge assumptions. Is this a threat
or a promise? And what can we do when our
assumptions are challenged—discuss them, defend them,
explore them, try to maintain the status quo, withdraw,
try to change the assumptions to fit our way of
thinking, or see differences as exciting and challenging
avenues toward growth?

A static system allows for no differences. A static
system gives the illusion of safety. A static system
ignores or disparages process in favor of content. A
static system devalues and devours itself.

Somehow, we must begin to realize that the
theology of our culture—White Male System
theology—forces us into a static system of hierarchy and
exploitation. We must begin to see how current
theological assumptions serve to perpetuate the White
Male System and limit human freedom and growth.

And now, let us begin.